Women Who Write

From the Past and the Present to the Future

Women Who Write

From the Past and the Present to the Future

Lucinda Irwin Smith

Julian Messner

...cinda Irwin Smith

...production in whole or in part in ...vision of Silver Burdett Press, Inc., ...Simon & Schuster, Inc., ...ll Bldg., Englewood Cliffs, NJ 07632.

JULIAN MESSNER and colophon are trademarks of Simon & Schuster, Inc. Design by Iris Weinstein. Manufactured in the United States of America.

(Lib. ed) 10 9 8 7 6 5 4 3 2 1
(Paper ed.) 10 9 8 7 6 5 4 3 2 1

The author would like to thank the following for their kind permission to reprint excerpts from these books:

Page 1, excerpt from *The Diary of Anaïs Nin, 1947–1955*, Volume 5, copyright © 1974 by Anaïs Nin, reprinted by permission of Harcourt Brace Jovanovich, Inc.

Pages 45 and 49, from *Anne Frank: The Diary of a Young Girl*, Doubleday & Company, New York, 1952.

Page 58, from *To Be Young, Gifted and Black: Lorraine Hansberry in Her Own Words*, adapted by Robert Nemiroff, © 1969. Reprinted by permission of the publisher, Prentice-Hall, Inc., Englewood Cliffs, New Jersey.

Pages 53 and 55, from *An Autobiography*, by Agatha Christie, Dodd, Mead & Company, Inc., New York, 1977.

Page 147, from *Letters to a Young Poet*, by Rainer Maria Rilke, translated by M. D. Herter Norton. By permission of W. W. Norton & Company, Inc. Copyright 1934 by W. W. Norton & Company, Inc. Renewed 1962 by M. D. Herter Norton. Copyright 1954 by W. W. Norton & Company, Inc. Copyright renewed 1982 by M. D. Herter Norton.

Page 43, excerpt from *To The Lighthouse* by Virginia Woolf, copyright 1927 by Harcourt Brace Jovanovich, Inc., renewed 1955 by Leonard Woolf, reprinted by permission of the publisher.

Library of Congress Cataloging-in-Publication Data

Smith, Lucinda.
Women who write.
Bibliography: p. 160
Includes index.
Summary: Discusses the nature and signature of authorship and uses interviews and biographical profiles to analyze the contributions of notable women writers.
1. Women and literature—United States. 2. Women and literature—Great Britain. 3. American literature—Women authors—History and criticism. 4. English literature—Women authors—History and criticism. 5. Women authors—Interviews. 6. Authorship [1. Women authors, American. 2. Women authors, English. 3. Authors, American. 4. Authors, English. 5. Authorship] I. Title.
PS147.S65 1989   810.9'9287   89-12290
ISBN 0-671-65668-6 (lib. bdg.)
ISBN 0-671-65669-4 (pbk.)

For Jeffrey

Acknowledgments

I am very grateful to these writers for their time, generous insights, and most of all, for agreeing to be interviewed: Dawn Garcia, Nikki Giovanni, Jan Goodwin, Beth Henley, Tama Janowitz, Maxine Hong Kingston, Norma Klein, Denise Levertov, Nancy Meyers, Joyce Carol Oates, Carolyn See, and Anne Tyler.

Contents

Introduction 1

1. *Why Write?* 3

2. *Women and Their Words* 7

3. *Writers from the Past* 13

    JANE AUSTEN 17
    GEORGE ELIOT 23
    EMILY DICKINSON 31
    VIRGINIA WOOLF 37
    ANNE FRANK 45
    AGATHA CHRISTIE 51
    LORRAINE
        HANSBERRY 57

4. *Contemporary Authors* 61

    DAWN GARCIA 65
    NIKKI GIOVANNI 75
    JAN GOODWIN 83
    BETH HENLEY 91

    TAMA JANOWITZ 97
    MAXINE HONG
        KINGSTON 103
    NORMA KLEIN 109
    DENISE LEVERTOV 117
    NANCY MEYERS 121
    JOYCE CAROL OATES 127
    CAROLYN SEE 131
    ANNE TYLER 139

5. *You, the Writer* 145

    MUST YOU WRITE? 146
    DEVELOPING YOUR
        GIFT 147
    THE WRITING
        PROCESS 152
    WHAT WILL YOU
        WRITE? 154
    THE WRITE TRAITS 156

Suggested Further
    Reading 160

Index 162

The role of the writer is not to say what we can all say but what we are unable to say.
ANAÏS NIN

Introduction

My father introduced me to the possibilities of language. A writer himself, he not only shared his love of books, but he presented the tools with which to create my own stories. My father's "job" was a solitary art; a craft. I can still recall the clicking of his manual typewriter as he worked late into the night. I knew there was something magical about his profession. Even when he appeared to be relaxing, he was hard at work, studying the world and transforming thoughts into wonderful words.

When I was eighteen, I met the author Irving Stone. He was seated in the center of an enormous department store, and he was signing copies of his latest book: *The Passions of the Mind.* When I expressed my desire to join his profession, he wrote these words on the inside cover of his book: "For Lucinda who is going to become a writer and one day will inscribe her book for me. Fraternally yours, Irving Stone." My fate had been decided.

I have always been intrigued by the lives of writers, and especially the lives of women writers throughout history. In this book, I have sought to examine such questions as why the women I profiled chose their craft, how their personal lives influenced their art, what obstacles they overcame to achieve their creative goals, and how they developed the discipline and drive necessary to write. I have tried to determine the unique combination of circumstance, ability, and destiny that shaped each individual and her work.

In these pages, you will discover some of the reasons that compel women to set pen to paper and put their ideas into words. Each writer from the past and each contemporary writer I interviewed chose this profession for complex and varied reasons. Some of the reasons are eloquent and dramatic, others are more prosaic. One writer claims writing is synonymous with breathing. Another writer admits frankly that writing was the only way she thought she could make a living.

I do not believe a woman's reasons for writing necessarily differ from those of a man. I simply wanted to concentrate on the lives and work of women writers. This book not only discusses the reasons why women write, but it also looks at how the profession of writing affects other aspects of a woman's life. The women profiled on these pages include poets, journalists, screenwriters, novelists, and playwrights. Many of these women have written in more than one genre.

If you want to become a writer, it is my hope that the ideas presented in these pages will help solidify your own very personal reasons for writing. I hope you'll be inspired to read more about all writers and to explore and develop your own unique gift. By studying the writers from the past and by examining the words of authors evaluating their craft today, you will gain additional insight into the infinite possibilities that come with the calling "to write."

I

Why Write?

Why do women write? For that matter, why does anyone write? What inner forces compel people to express their ideas in written words?

Throughout history, various analysts (who are themselves writers) have put forth hundreds of theories to answer this question. People write to assert control over their world, to express opinions, to create a new reality, to escape the old reality, to gain power, to become immortal, and…

A writer is a teacher and an entertainer. A writer consoles, provokes, amuses, angers, and encourages the reader to think, fantasize, and act. A writer ignites the reader's imagination.

The writer serves as an interpreter of reality. The writer sways opinion, creates heroes and heroines, and defines love, courage, happiness, and tragedy.

But what audacity the writer has! How can anyone presume to take on the powerful role of interpreter? What are the requirements and the qualifications? Quite simply, there are no formal qualifications, and the desire to express an idea is the only requirement.

Certain professions are limited by age. Physical capabilities play a significant role in determining the duration of an athlete's or a dancer's career. But a person can begin writing at the age of eight or eighty-five. Life is the writer's school. Therefore age, and the insight that comes with years, works as an advantage to the writer.

Romantic images commonly associated with the life of an artist can lure a person into a writing career. The word *writer* conjures up images of Ernest Hemingway, Gertrude Stein, Sylvia Plath, Lillian Hellman, and others. The fantasy of sitting in a dark café discussing art, philosophy, and literature may attract a person to the Hollywood picture of a writer's life. For some, writers are defined as intelligent, eccentric, individualistic, creative, and witty.

But is the desire to be regarded as artistic or eccentric all that's necessary to write? Perhaps momentarily, but ultimately the love of language and the yearning to tell one's story must be strong enough to justify the incredibly hard work a career in writing demands.

Writing enables a creative person to verbalize his or her impressions of the life experience. Each individual's version of reality is different. Do women write differently from men? Only in the sense that each individual, regardless of sex, has a different story to tell. Experience, rather than sex, determines what and how someone writes. Because of the different sociological histories of men and women, literature often reflects a distinctly female or male point of view. Unfortunately, women have not always had the freedom or the opportunity to write. Oppression based on sex, religion, or race has proved a strong motivating force for the formation and expression of ideas throughout history.

Many writers admit they hate the actual process of writing. They dread the blank piece of paper and the endless hours of reworking a sentence or a paragraph until it's perfect. Why then do writers return day after day to the torture of the empty page? A famous cliché claims "there's a novel inside everyone just waiting to be written." The majority of these stories will remain locked in the hearts of humanity forever. An individual becomes a writer when some inexplicable urge forces his or her story out of the mind and into words. A writer confronts his or her self, and the truth about his or her existence.

While there are risks involved, there are also many rewards. If you are not deterred by the contradictions of this calling, sharpen your pencil and get started.

2

Women and Their Words

If Shakespeare had had a sister with literary aspirations, would her life have had a happy ending? Virginia Woolf poses this question in her feminist essay *A Room of One's Own*. Woolf speculates that if such a woman had lived and had been as gifted as her brother, she would have endured a life of extreme frustration and unhappiness. Not content with a marriage arranged by her parents, Ms. Shakespeare would most likely have run away. Then, completely alone in the world and unable to find work, she would have seen only one escape: suicide.

While such a sibling did not exist, so far as we know, Woolf's pathetic description eloquently captures the probable plight of a woman who possessed great literary or creative gifts in the sixteenth century. Woolf goes on to speculate that had such a woman actually found it within herself to publish a poem, sonnet, or essay, she most likely would have used the pseudonym "anonymous." Is it possible, as Woolf suggests, that some of history's great "anonymous" literature was actually written by women? The answer is yes. It is a fact that many women writers assumed masculine pen names or remained anonymous. These women often led secret lives, writing in obscurity, while pretending their talents were suited only to raising children, darning socks, and keeping house. The identities of some of these writers have been revealed. How many others took their secret to their graves?

If one asks, "Why do women write?" it seems only logical to wonder, "What took them so long?" Why didn't women begin writing when men first discovered the value of the written word?

Even if a woman had yearned to tell her story, her lack of education would have proved frustrating when she attempted to put her tale in writing. Only the nobility were able to read and write, and it was deemed "inappropriate" for a genteel lady to pass the time in such creative pursuits. Perhaps an equally significant handicap facing women was the lack of an audience. Who would have read the outpourings of a woman's heart? Unfortunately, literary works by women were not in great demand.

Aphra Behn (1640–1689) has become legendary as the first woman in England to make a living as a writer. There are several important reasons why Behn and other women began writing for profit. Education was becoming accessible to the middle class. Although women aristocrats had been instructed in the classics since the 1500s, the 1600s offered a more practical and useful education. During this period, men were also writing a greater number of popular works, and women readers formed a large percentage of every successful author's following.

Many of the favorite novels of the mid-1700s feature the antics of colorful heroines. It was perhaps inevitable that women would one day write novels about their fantasies as well as their everyday experiences. As letter-writing occupied a significant portion of many middle class women's daily life, it followed that some of their first novels, such as Fanny Burney's *Evelina,* would be "epistolary," or written in the form of letters.

Middle class women also took up the pen for a very fundamental reason: Money. Writing offered a relatively pleasant and sometimes lucrative way to earn a living. A woman could support herself and her children or add to the total family income with the wages from her art.

Any female author willing to subject her work to public scrutiny was almost certain to draw criticism. Some literary scholars have suggested that early women writers needed not only perseverance but great courage to succeed in their craft. The world of letters was dominated by men. Consequently, a sensitive female novelist was almost guaranteed to have her feelings bruised when she entered the somewhat hostile arena of writing. When Mary Wollstonecraft (1759–1797) published her feminist book *A Vindication of the Rights of Woman,* one male critic called her "a hyena in petticoats."

When women writers realized they could survive the hostility, earn a living, and receive recognition for their work, they began to gain confidence and discover their own voices. Until this time, images of the female sex in literature had all been created by men. All the great heroines in literature, from Chaucer's Wife of Bath to Shakespeare's Juliet, had been written solely from a male perspective. Now women writers had the opportunity to create characters and tell stories in their words, from their point of view.

As women writers became more prolific in England, their contemporaries in the new colonies also took up the pen. By 1820, nearly one-third of all American novels had been written by women. In addition, women began to write about social injustice. During the 1800s, women were not allowed to vote. In many communities, women were not even permitted to speak in public. Writing was therefore a way to voice an opinion to a large group of people. Women wrote about abuses in marriage, the hardships of working in factories, and the evils of slavery. Harriet Beecher Stowe's famous novel *Uncle Tom's Cabin* (1851) helped awaken the public to the horrors of slavery.

While some women were writing about social wrongs or

writing fiction, other women were keeping diaries and journals of their struggle to cross the continent in covered wagons. Between 1840 and 1870, a quarter of a million Americans left the security of the Eastern cities for the promises of the West. Over eight hundred diaries and journals have been published or preserved in library collections. Women wrote to overcome loneliness, homesickness, and fear. They told of the perils of the weather, the harsh beauty of the land, and the hardships of childbirth and raising a family. These diaries provide an accurate account of pioneer life. Although some of these diaries were published in newspapers, the stories did not deter other adventurous women from heading West.

The dawn of the twentieth century further awakened the consciousness of both men and women and previewed many forthcoming changes. Women used their literary abilities to voice opinions on such controversial subjects as birth control, the vote, female psychology, and female sexuality. New questions were raised, and the issues about which to write became as numerous as the women who chose the written word as a way to express their ideas.

After struggling for many centuries to gain respect and recognition for their work, by the early 1900s women writers had successfully penetrated almost every genre of literature.

The early novelist Aphra Behn once described the creative side of her personality as her "masculine part." Because of Behn and the female writers who followed her, however, women developed confidence in their literary voices and no longer felt obliged to excuse, justify, or defend the artistic aspect of their beings. Through their words, women began to explore and challenge their culture, their identity, and their future.

Between 1909 and 1966, six women, representing a wide spectrum of ethnic backgrounds and philosophical viewpoints, were awarded the Nobel Prize in Literature: 1909, Selma

Lagerlöf (Sweden); 1926, Grazia Deledda (Italy); 1928, Sigrid Undset (Norway); 1938, Pearl Buck (United States); 1945, Gabriela Mistral (Chile); 1966, Nelly Sachs (Germany). Women had indeed proved to themselves and to the world they had something to say. As a result, aspiring young writers of both sexes could look beyond Shakespeare, Milton, and other male authors for role models. A great tradition of literature had been established through the life and work of such writers as Charlotte and Emily Brontë, Elizabeth Barrett Browning, George Sand, Edith Wharton, Gertrude Stein, Zora Neale Hurston, Isak Dinesen, Anaïs Nin, and countless others. In the following chapter, the lives of several diverse female authors are profiled for their unique part in the history of women and their words.

3

Writers from the Past

*T*he lives of seven women writers are profiled on the following pages. Although they lived at different times in history and were separate and unique individuals, the fact that all seven expressed their ideas through writing prompts this question: What, if any, similarities can be found among this random selection of three novelists, one mystery writer, one poet, one playwright, and one diarist?

Only a brief investigation into the biographies of these writers is necessary to reveal that each woman possessed an acute awareness of herself and her environment. Even at an early age, these women began to question themselves and the world around them.

For these women, a seemingly instinctive desire to analyze their surroundings found an outlet in writing. Whether in essays, poetry, or prose, these writers worked out their questions through fictional situations and nonfictional essays, as well as through personal and sometimes very private letters and diaries.

Each of these women possessed an exceptional intellect and the initiative to expand her knowledge. Whether educated at home or at school, each woman was raised to appreciate the value of learning. A certain curiosity was instilled in each writer as a child, and she was encouraged to further her knowledge through reading.

All seven writers had strong parents, and in particular, strong fathers. In addition to having important relationships with their *mothers, five of these women—Jane Austen, Emily Dickinson, Virginia Woolf, Anne Frank, and Agatha Christie—also formed close and lasting bonds with their sisters.*

Austen, George Eliot, Woolf, Christie, and Lorraine Hansberry were "professionals" in the sense that they were paid for their work. With the exception of Dickinson (Frank hoped to become a professional writer), an important aspect of these women's need to question was the desire to share their ideas and be reinforced through publication and recognition.

The need to create, as a way to express one's being, was evidenced even in the early writings of these women. All of these writers, with the exception of Anne Frank, succeeded in fulfilling at least a significant portion of their creative potential. Although Anne Frank was not allowed time to realize the extent of her ability, she was nevertheless aware of this yearning. Her love of writing gave her the power and the hope to endure the devastation of her young life. For this reason, Anne Frank is a unique addition to this group of women. She personifies the overwhelming desire to create. Even in the face of unbelievable obstacles, her voice could not be silenced.

Finally, even among her own circle of family, friends, and readers, each of these women stood out as exceptional. Through their words, generations of readers will continue to look at life, find answers, and ask new questions.

THE NATIONAL PORTRAIT GALLERY, LONDON

Jane Austen

Jane Austen

By what standards is a book judged to be a classic? In general, a book receives this accolade when it maintains its appeal for generations of readers.

Jane Austen's *Pride and Prejudice* is such a book. Although the novel is set in the early 1800s, the themes are universal and timeless. Through situations played out by her characters, Jane Austen comments on love, money, the institution of marriage, the separation of the classes, and the pretensions of the clergy and the aristocracy. She observes the behavior of polite society with a keen wit and a mixture of irony, comedy, and satire. Although readers may grin at the foibles of Austen's characters, they are ultimately taking a closer look at themselves and at their own social interactions.

The novels of Jane Austen have always had particular appeal because of her keen observations of the plight of middle class women. Like herself, female members of the gentry were regarded as commodities in the marriage marketplace. Through characters such as Elizabeth and Jane Bennet in *Pride and Prejudice,* Austen explored the frustrations of intelligent women forced to live in a society that placed enormous restrictions on personal choice and educational opportunity. She sympathized with her sex and regretted that women were dependent upon men for a sense of identity as well as for financial support.

Although most women of her era lived within very rigid boundaries, Jane Austen found an outlet for her unique analytical genius. She could stand back from her world and translate observations of reality into fictional masterpieces.

Given the enormous popularity her novels enjoy today, it is difficult to comprehend that during her lifetime Austen remained virtually unknown to her readers. Although her books sold well, Jane Austen's enormous talent was never publicly acknowledged. On the cover of her novel *Sense and Sensibility*, the author is simply referred to as "A Lady." Her family and friends were very aware of her writing abilities, but she described herself modestly as "the most unlearned and uninformed female who ever dared to be an authoress."

Jane Austen was born on December 16, 1775, in the southwest region of England known as Hampshire. Her father, George Austen, was a minister and a schoolteacher. She had six brothers and one sister. At the age of seven, Jane was sent away to school with her older sister, Cassandra. When the girls returned a few years later, they continued their education under their father's supervision. Jane read all the classics and was also fond of poetry. The entire family enjoyed novels and read them aloud to one another. They delighted in performing theatrical plays, converting their barn into a theater and enlisting their cousins' participation in the performances. Perhaps Jane's involvement in these plays first encouraged her interest in writing. By the age of twelve, she was writing prologues for the performances. She also wrote rhymed charades and a series of pieces dedicated to members of her family. She copied them all into three notebooks entitled "Volume the First," "Volume the Second," and "Volume the Third." These early pieces reveal Jane's humor and talent for parody.

The Austens socialized a great deal, attending parties given by local gentry, and much of the insight Jane gained into middle class manners was from first-hand experience.

Like many young women of her era, Jane Austen was a

prolific letter-writer. Scholars have gained insight into her development as a writer through her correspondence with her sister. The sisters exchanged letters while they were visiting their married brothers or other friends throughout the countryside. Although Cassandra destroyed many of Jane's letters after her death, scholars have still been able to see glimpses of her unique wit in those that have remained. Some critics have accused Jane of being rather insensitive, however, and somewhat condescending to her friends and acquaintances.

Although neither Jane nor Cassandra married, they both were involved in numerous flirtations as young women. As they grew older, both fell in love. Unfortunately, their relationships either ended in disappointment or in tragedy.

As Jane indicates in her novels, especially in *Pride and Prejudice,* money was of prime importance when planning a "suitable" marriage. The first young man for whom Jane developed a fondness could not marry her because neither possessed an inheritance or an income. Cassandra was engaged to a man who died of yellow fever in the West Indies. He was serving as chaplain to a regiment of British troops.

In 1795, when she was twenty, Jane began writing "Elinor and Marianne" (it later received the title *Sense and Sensibility*). As soon as she completed her work, it was read to the family, who thought it excellent. Thus encouraged, she began "First Impressions" (later titled *Pride and Prejudice*). In 1798, Jane began yet another work, "Susan." It was renamed *Northanger Abbey* and published after her death. Jane's family were sincere believers in her talent. Her father once wrote to a publisher about "First Impressions." Unfortunately, the publisher never responded.

Although still unpublished, Jane continued to write and pursue the multitude of activities available through her large and growing family. In 1802, when she was twenty-seven, she received a proposal of marriage from the twenty-one-year-old son of a family friend. She accepted, but after a restless night she changed her mind and rejected the possibility of spending her life as Mrs. Harris Bigg-Wither.

In 1803, Jane's novel *Susan* was sold to a publisher named Crosby for a small sum of money. Jane's brother Henry had evidently arranged the sale and had not revealed the author's identity. But though the book was advertised in a publication entitled *Flowers of Literature,* it was never printed by Crosby.

Following the death of George Austen in 1805, the family suffered financial hardships, and it became necessary for the Austen brothers to supplement their mother's and sisters' income. The three women eventually settled in Chawton cottage, on land owned by Jane's wealthy brother Edward.

In 1809, Jane, hoping to keep her identity secret, used the assumed name of "Mrs. Ashton Dennis" in a letter to Crosby about her book. Six years had passed, and she thought perhaps he had lost it. Crosby replied that although he had no intention of publishing *Susan,* he nevertheless owned the rights. He threatened to sue anyone who published the book, but he said he would sell the book back to its author. Unfortunately, because of the family's poor financial situation, Jane was in no position to buy back the book.

At the age of thirty-four, "Aunt Jane" was described by a niece as being pretty, but dressing in rather plain, middle-aged clothing. She always wore a cap that partly concealed her dark brown curly hair. Jane, Cassandra, and Mrs. Austen excelled at needlework and also made beautiful quilts. Jane was a great favorite among her nieces and nephews, and the cottage at Chawton was frequently occupied with visiting relatives.

Finally, in 1811, Thomas Egerton, of the Military Library, Whitehall, agreed to publish *Sense and Sensibility.* If any loss was incurred, the "authoress" was expected to reimburse the publisher. Fortunately, this proved unnecessary as the book was well received and sold very well. The first edition sold out in eighteen months, and Jane earned a sizable profit. The author's identity was, of course, not revealed. In November of 1812, *Pride and Prejudice* was sold to Egerton; it was published in January of 1813 in an edition of 1500 copies. By November, a second printing was already available. In 1814, *Mansfield Park* was published by Egerton, and the first edition sold out quickly.

In 1815, Jane changed publishers. Mr. John Murray of Albemarle Street (who was also Byron's publisher) published *Emma* in that year. After the publication of *Emma,* Jane's brother Henry bought *Susan* back from Crosby. Only after the transaction had been completed did Henry reveal to Crosby that the author of the enormously succcessful *Pride and Prejudice* was also the author of *Susan.* Meanwhile, in August of 1815, Jane began her novel *Persuasion.*

Many of Jane's relatives hoped to follow in the footsteps of their literary "Aunt Jane," and she devoted many hours to commenting on their manuscripts. By late 1815, Jane's health had begun to fail, and in April of 1817, she made out her will. With the exception of a few small items, she left everything to Cassandra. Modern physicians have tentatively diagnosed her illness as Addison's disease. This illness results in the deterioration of the adrenal glands. It is characterized by extreme weakness, weight loss, and brownish patches on the skin.

Jane Austen died on Friday, July 18, 1817. She was forty-two. After his sister's death, Henry arranged for *Persuasion* and *Northanger Abbey* (originally called *Susan*) to be published. Henry wrote a "Biographical Notice of the Author," in which Jane Austen was identified for the first time. From that moment on, her reputation continued to grow, and eventually she achieved a prominent place in the history of literature. The woman who began in anonymity has gained immortality.

George Eliot

George Eliot

The work of George Eliot holds a significant place in the history of literature. Most especially, it represents a critical link in the development of the novel. Some scholars consider Eliot one of the first modern novelists. Rather than advancing her plots primarily by means of the outward behavior of her characters, Eliot penetrated the inner psychology of her heroes and heroines in an attempt to understand human nature.

Eliot's novels were considered more intellectual than those that were written earlier. She successfully blended philosophy with fiction and thus allowed her characters to grapple with ethical, spiritual, and moral dilemmas. Contemporary audiences continue to enjoy Eliot's novels. While being drawn into the life-style and landscape of nineteenth-century England, the modern reader is challenged through humor, sensitivity, and insight to ponder the timeless puzzles of the human intellect.

One of the great novelists who assumed a masculine pseudonym (such as Charlotte and Emily Brontë, who wrote as Currer and Ellis Bell, and Amandine Aurore Dudevant, who was known as George Sand), George Eliot came into the world with the name Mary Ann Evans. Although her first book wasn't published until she was thirty-eight, as a young woman she began to explore the great psychological, religious, and social themes that would appear in her fiction.

Mary Ann Evans was born on November 22, 1819. Her family lived in a town called Chilvers Coton, in the Midlands of

England. Her father, Robert Evans, worked as a land agent for Francis Newdigate, a wealthy aristocrat. In this capacity he managed the estate and supervised the mining and agricultural interests of his employer. Robert Evans was a man of strong character who had a reputation for great physical strength. He had a powerful influence on Mary Ann. She would later model her character Adam Bede in the novel of the same name, as well as *Middlemarch's* Caleb Garth, on her father. She had enormous respect for Robert Evans, and she admired his principles of honor, hard work, discipline, and responsibility.

Mary Ann's mother, Christiana Pearson, tended to dominate her husband, partly because her social background was somewhat superior to his. Besides Mary Ann, the couple had two older children: Christiana (born in 1814) and Isaac (1816). At the age of five, Mary Ann was sent away to school along with her sister. Her most powerful memories of this experience were of horrible nightmares and of always being cold. The nightmares that began in childhood would plague Mary Ann throughout her life. In spite of these negative aspects of school, she developed a great love of books. Reading material was scarce, however, and Mary Ann virtually memorized some of her favorite books, including *Aesop's Fables* and *The Pilgrim's Progress*. At the age of seven, she discovered the work of Sir Walter Scott. His novel *Waverley* was an early favorite, and Scott became an important influence on her developing mind.

Even at an early age, Mary Ann saw herself as plain and believed she was a disappointment to her mother. At Miss Franklin's school in Coventry, her strong religious feelings were awakened. In addition to being a superior student in school, she organized prayer meetings and devoted many hours to helping poor citizens in the local town. The other students were somewhat in awe of her intelligence. She also played the piano, and her teachers looked forward to reading her excellent essays.

Mary Ann enjoyed school, and she was greatly disappointed when her mother's illness forced her to return home. Mrs. Evans died soon thereafter, and because her older sister had married, Mary Ann had to take over the housekeeping duties. Because of the excellence she'd demonstrated at school, however, several of her teachers journeyed to her home to give her private lessons.

Even though she was able to escape through reading, Mary Ann felt frustrated and lonely. She began to develop serious headaches, which would recur throughout her life. Her one great pleasure was exchanging letters with a former teacher, Miss Maria Lewis. Mary Ann offered opinions on current fiction and religious novels. She also sent Miss Lewis several of her verses. They would later appear in a Christian publication under the initials M.A.E.

Finally, in 1841, Mary Ann was able to leave "Griff," the family home. As Robert Evans was nearing his seventies, he felt it was time to retire. Isaac was left in charge of his father's business. Mary Ann and Robert moved to "Bird Grove," a beautiful house near Coventry. Through their acquaintances, Mary Ann met Charles Bray, a Unitarian and a social activist. His progressive ideas greatly challenged Mary Ann's Evangelical Christian beliefs. At his home, Mary Ann had the opportunity to meet such great thinkers as Ralph Waldo Emerson. When she realized that her new ideas were in conflict with traditional Christian values, she decided to stop attending church. This decision caused a serious rift with her father. Although she eventually resumed her church attendance, her religious beliefs had undergone a dramatic and permanent change. Her philosophy now centered around a doctrine she referred to as "truth of feeling."

Through Charles Bray and his wife, Mary Ann became acquainted with the German scholar Dr. Robert Henry Brabant. His daughter had recently married Mrs. Bray's brother, Charles Hennell. Through this connection, she received the assignment of translating David Friedrich Strauss's *Das Leben Jesu* (The Life of Jesus) from German to English. This was Mary Ann's first published work. It took three years to complete, and was published by Chapman Brothers of London.

In 1849, Robert Evans died. The loss had a devastating effect on Mary Ann, and in an attempt to console her, the Brays suggested she join them for a trip abroad. After visiting Avignon, Marseilles, and Genoa, Mary Ann decided to stay on in Geneva. She rented a room in the home of Monsieur and Madame François D'Albert-Durade. Durade, a well-known artist, was only four feet tall. He painted her portrait, and they established a devoted friendship. He would later translate several of her novels into French.

After experimenting with a variety of different names, Mary Ann eventually decided upon Marian. Armed with her new identity, she left Geneva and returned to London. She hoped to find lodging with her publisher, John Chapman, who ran a boarding house above his office. Chapman's home was a meeting place for many intellectuals. Although Chapman lived with both his wife and his mistress, it appears he may have also been romantically involved with Marian. The other women soon became jealous of her presence, and she left for six months. When she returned, Marian began working on Chapman's radical quarterly magazine, the *Westminster Review*. It was through Chapman that Marian met the philosopher Herbert Spencer. They developed an important friendship. In 1853, Spencer introduced Marian to George Henry Lewes, the editor of a radical weekly and the author of *The Biographical History of Philosophy*.

Lewes was regarded as an unattractive man. In fact, one of his nicknames was "the ape." He was also known for a lack of manners and for discussing controversial subjects in polite company. In spite of these qualities, Lewes was a brilliant thinker and knowledgeable in many areas including law, medicine, philosophy, and literature. Although he was married, he believed in "free love." Lewes had three children with his wife, and she had two children with another man. Soon after Marian and Lewes met, they left England and went to Germany. Their relationship would last for twenty-four years. But, though they wanted to marry, Lewes was never able to obtain a divorce.

When the couple returned from Berlin, Marian began working as the editor of the "Belles Lettres" section of the *Westminster Review*. Although she contributed several essays, her identity remained anonymous. One of her articles was entitled "Silly Novels by Lady Novelists."

Money was scarce for Marian and George, as he was still obligated to support his wife and three children, as well as his wife's other children. Although Marian was somewhat uneasy about the relationship, she used the title "Mrs." and hoped outsiders would regard it as a marriage. However, when Isaac learned of it, he decided to have nothing more to do with his sister, and he insisted the family follow his example.

Though distressed by Isaac's cruelty, Marian was curious about the possibilities of writing fiction. She attempted the first chapter of a novel and showed it to Lewes. His reaction was cautious, yet he encouraged her to continue writing. In her journal entry dated September 23, 1855, Marian noted that she had begun to write "The Sad Fortunes of the Reverend Amos Barton." When Lewes read the finished manuscript, they both began to cry. Taking upon himself the role of literary editor, Lewes contacted John Blackwood of Edinburgh. Believing it to be the work of a clergyman, Blackwood agreed to publish the story in *Blackwood's Magazine*. He showed the piece to the novelist William Makepeace Thackeray, who indicated he'd like to see more of the author's work. Thackeray was an esteemed member of Blackwood's literary circle, and a close personal friend. On February 4, 1857, Marian informed Blackwood that the author of "Amos Barton" had selected a *nom de plume:* George Eliot. She later acknowledged that "George" was in honor of Lewes, and that she simply liked the sound of "Eliot." In January 1858, "Amos Barton" was published as a book, and several copies were sent to eminent writers. Charles Dickens suspected the author was a woman.

Marian continued to write, and in 1859, *Adam Bede* appeared in print. Although Blackwood discovered the identity of George Eliot, he believed that disclosure of her domestic situation would greatly harm book sales. Marian remained anonymous, and the book became an immediate success.

Lewes was a great admirer of Jane Austen's novels, and he insisted Marian read all her books. They read the novels aloud to one another. Although she respected Austen's work, Marian preferred the novels of Charlotte and Emily Brontë, Harriet Beecher Stowe, and George Sand.

People were gradually beginning to guess George Eliot's true identity. Lewes tried to protect Marian from any cruel gossip. It was difficult to deny the truth, however, because many of the details and characters in *Adam Bede* were closely linked to reality.

The Mill on the Floss was published in 1860. Some of the reviews were obviously influenced by the revelation that the author was living with a man to whom she was not married. But in spite of several negative reviews, most people greatly admired the book. Nevertheless, Marian was excluded from "society." When she and Lewes entertained on Saturday evenings, male guests frequently called without their wives. Fortunately, Marian had little time for parties as she was busy writing her next book, *Silas Marner.* It was published in 1861. *Romola* followed, and it was published as a serial in 1862. *Felix Holt, the Radical* is often considered her least successful novel. It took fourteen months to write and was published in 1866. Having written so many books, Marian decided to pause in her fiction writing and compose verse instead.

Her next appearance as a novelist was with her masterpiece, *Middlemarch,* published in 1871. This book's financial success greatly alleviated the Leweses' monetary difficulties. Queen Victoria was one of George Eliot's greatest admirers, and interestingly enough, she did not frown on Marian's relationship with Lewes.

Daniel Deronda appeared in 1876. At about this time, as Marian's health began to deteriorate, it became clear that Lewes was gravely ill. On November 13, 1878, he died. Less than one year after his death, Marian married John Walter Cross, a man twenty years her junior. In 1869, Marian and George had met Cross while he and his mother were traveling in Europe. Cross became their friend and broker and helped the Leweses locate a house. When Lewes died, Johnny became very attentive, and gradually his friendship with Marian became romantic. They were married on May 6, 1880. They honeymooned in Venice and traveled throughout Austria and Germany. In September, Marian's kidney problems recurred. She soon developed a sore throat, and her kidney condition worsened. On December 22, 1880, at the age of sixty-one, she died.

Marian was buried beside Lewes at Highgate Cemetery. Although her popularity declined after her death, by the mid 1900s George Eliot was recognized as a great writer whose literary works rank alongside those of Charles Dickens, William Makepeace Thackeray, and Henry James.

Emily Dickinson

Emily Dickinson

> This is my letter to the World
> That never wrote to Me—

Emily Dickinson was a poet of many paradoxes. Although she chose not to communicate with the world during her lifetime, she seemed to have a premonition that someday her "letter" would be read.

At the time of her death in 1886, only twelve of Dickinson's poems had been published. Her family and close friends knew she wrote poetry, but the bounty they discovered tucked beneath a bureau drawer was truly astounding. Dickinson had written 1,775 poems. Only twelve of them were titled and few were dated. Although she'd bound many of the poems together in little booklets, most were written on odd bits of paper or included in letters.

At first glance, Emily Dickinson appears to be the extreme stereotype of a reclusive spinster. She never married. She lived with her sister Lavinia, who also never married, in the house where they had been raised. Together they cared for their aging parents.

In her later years, Dickinson dressed all in white and rarely ventured outside the house. Her companions were Lavinia and her menagerie of cats.

While the surface details seem to paint the classic portrait of a lonely, eccentric woman, one must look deeper in order to see the true picture. These elements, which may appear "uneventful," were just the ingredients necessary to create a world beyond the constraints of ordinary life. Perhaps, for a woman like Dickinson, these factors can provide the ideal conditions for the creation of art.

Emily Elizabeth Dickinson was born in Amherst, Massachusetts, on December 10, 1830. The Dickinsons lived in a stately mansion and held a prominent position in society. Dickinson's grandfather was one of the founders of Amherst College. Her father, Edward Dickinson, served as treasurer of the college and was also elected to one term in Congress. Emily was the middle of three children—she had a younger sister and an older brother, Austin. Emily was educated at Amherst Academy and Mount Holyoke Female Seminary.

Her mother, Emily Norcross Dickinson, was a quiet, reclusive woman who remained somewhat of a stranger to her children. She was frequently ill and often depressed. Edward Dickinson traveled a great deal and also maintained a distant relationship with his children. Mrs. Dickinson lived until the age of seventy-eight, and it was only in her last years that she and Emily achieved a degree of closeness. Because they lacked a strong emotional bond with their parents, the children turned to one another for love. For the duration of their lives, Lavinia and Emily lived together, and Austin lived next door with his wife and family.

Emily Dickinson left behind many riddles. In searching for their solutions, one can begin to understand why she wrote and why she sought the answers to certain questions.

Dickinson wrote because she loved language. Very early in life she became aware of the power of words. She was an avid letter-writer, and often made preliminary drafts of her correspondence. While she wrote letters to communicate, she also took the opportunity to experiment with language and fine-tune her writing. She once wrote to a friend, Joseph Lyman, that words "glowed" on the page like "sapphires."

The more Dickinson became aware of the power of words and the worlds that existed within them, the greater the role they began to play in her life. For her, words would eventually become a substitute for companionship, romantic love, marriage, travel, and even God.

Very early in her life, Emily began to question humankind's relationship with God. This battle would become a dominant theme in many of her poems. Religion was a powerful force in the small communities of western Massachusetts, and the Bible was read every day in the Dickinson household. Conversion, or the conscious decision to submit one's will, thought, and deed to God, was considered a necessary rite of passage. Although Emily Dickinson watched her family and friends undergo this spiritual change, she stayed in the background, stubbornly unyielding, determined to remain a loner.

Although she remained skeptical of God's forgiveness and love, Dickinson was a firm believer in God's existence. However, she was unable to perceive God as a caring entity. She felt His dealings with humanity were cruel and unsympathetic. Death was an everyday occurrence. Emily Dickinson lost many friends to untimely and painful deaths through childbirth, disease, and accidents. There was no anesthetic and few cures for serious illness. People often died when a cold turned into pneumonia. Between 1851 and 1854, thirty-three friends and acquaintances of the Dickinson family died.

In addition, many of Dickinson's childhood acquaintances married and moved hundreds of miles away. Separation through death or distance became an important theme in Dickinson's work. Through her writing, she overcame her fears. In words, there would be no death, no separation, no abandonment, and no disappointment. And while there might also be no eternal life in heaven, she pondered the possibility of immortality through the "breath" of her poetry.

Dickinson's fear of separation and loss contributed to her self-imposed exile. Rather than surrounding herself with people to overcome her fears, she shut out human contact and surrounded herself with words. Privacy was the only complete protection and ultimately the safest fortress.

If one looks further into Dickinson's fear of separation, one senses an even greater fear: Separation from self. By refusing religion and marriage, she avoided the two things that would have required her to give up a part of her identity.

In rejecting the possible "selves" presented by nineteenth-century society, Dickinson made sure she would not be identified as "religious" or as a wife or mother. But there is ample evidence that she fell in love several times during her life.

Her greatest expression of love can be found in what have been called the "Master" poems. Scholars have tried for decades to uncover the identity of the person to whom these poems are addressed. Although the name is locked away forever, there is little doubt that the "Master" evoked in Dickinson a strong and painful passion. For unknown reasons, this love was not returned. Therefore, in love Emily Dickinson once again experienced the pain of human separation. The "Master" poems and most of her romantic verses are dominated by the theme of unrequited love.

Dickinson fell in love again at the age of forty-eight. Judge Otis P. Lord was a man with whom she'd had a long acquaintance. Their friendship became serious, and he proposed marriage. For a variety of reasons that included her mother's illness, Dickinson put off making a decision until Lord's death settled the question.

Dickinson also established many strong friendships with men through her correspondence. Although she presented a quiet and shy demeanor in person, when she was safe behind the fortress of language Dickinson had the confidence to write letters to many famous and powerful men. Thomas Wentworth Higginson was a Unitarian minister and widely read essayist. In 1862, Dickinson read his "Letter to a Young Contributor." This article, which appeared in *The Atlantic Monthly,* encouraged the efforts of young writers. She wrote to him and they began a lifelong correspondence. She only met Higginson twice, but she included more than one hundred poems in her letters to him.

Though Dickinson first introduced herself to Higginson as a novice poet, she had in fact been writing for several years. Why did so few of her poems appear in print during her lifetime? It may have been tied to her wish for fame after her death, or perhaps it was because Higginson and those around her never seriously encouraged her to pursue publication. She made a point on several occasions of denying the importance of having her work published, claiming that publishing her poetry would be similar to selling her mind.

During the 1800s, several women authors were widely read and treated as celebrities. From what we know of Emily Dickinson, celebrity is not a notion she would have welcomed. Dickinson was undoubtedly more afraid of losing her privacy than of facing the public scrutiny publication might have caused.

When Thomas Wentworth Higginson met Emily Dickinson for the first time, the woman who emerged from her cocoon was very different from the woman he had come to know through her letters and poetry. In a letter to his wife, Higginson described Dickinson as a "plain little woman."

Perhaps Higginson knew that within this diminutive, quiet woman there existed another, brilliant identity. Through the gift of words she left the world, readers will forever see the possibilities Emily Dickinson sensed within herself: Passion, wisdom, power, and infinite beauty.

THE NATIONAL PORTRAIT GALLERY, LONDON

Virginia Woolf

Virginia Woolf

Why are so many people drawn to the life and work of Virginia Woolf? This delicate, ethereal woman with her classic features, long white fingers, and loose-fitting gowns has become the symbol of a legendary moment in literary history. As both a woman and an artist, Woolf attempted to free herself from the constraints of society, her upbringing, her expectations, her emotional disorders, and her sex. Perhaps it is because people identify with her struggles that she has gained such a following. Her admirers not only read her works but they continue to probe the real-life details of her world and the people who lived in it.

Woolf possessed a brilliant imagination as well as a gift for satire and social observation. She was a prolific fiction writer and a respected literary historian and critic. She had a loyal circle of fascinating and brilliant friends. Her husband and sister adored her, and her writing brought financial security and critical acclaim. At fifty-nine, she had acquired the intellectual and material trappings of a successful writer.

Why then was her soul so tortured? And why were the "voices" within her mind able to take control of her fragile genius and lead her to the banks of the River Ouse, where she filled her pockets with rocks and drowned? The demons that drove Woolf mad competed with the creative forces that enabled her to write. These opposing energies were always near confrontation, and when they collided, her manic-depressive symptoms emerged and the destructive powers of her mind took control. Whenever she neared completion of a novel, she suffered such an ordeal. Her emotions, still raw from weeks of heightened creativity, became increasingly vulnerable and unpredictable. Any stability or confidence she might have gained from her outpouring of work was shattered by her delusions. Medical experts suggest that had Virginia Woolf lived today, her illness might have been treated by medication. She lived in a time, however, when psychological illnesses were not understood and were consequently feared. Virginia Woolf lived with the awareness that her attacks would recur all her life. And because she could do nothing to prevent them, she dreaded the day the "voices" might take over and become victorious.

In addition to whatever genetic factors contributed to her personality, Virginia Woolf was the product of a unique environment. She lived at a decisive moment in literary and political history. She divided her time between the intellectual atmosphere of London's Bloomsbury district and the picturesque beauty of the English countryside, and she surrounded herself with a rare clique of artists and eccentrics who influenced her development as a writer and as an individual.

Virginia Woolf came from a large and very literate family. Her father, whose first wife was the daughter of William Makepeace Thackeray, found himself a widower at a relatively early age. Sir Leslie Stephen soon married a beautiful young widow with three children. Sir Leslie and Julia Duckworth had four children: Vanessa, born 1879; Thoby, 1880; Virginia, 1882; and Adrian, 1883. Virginia was born on January 25.

Sir Leslie Stephen was a well-known man of letters. He achieved literary recognition as the editor of the *Dictionary of National Biography*. Virginia enjoyed the use of her father's extensive library. Because she could not receive the education afforded young men of her era, she was forced to enhance her knowledge through determination and self-discipline.

In 1895, Virginia's mother died, and the event had devastating consequences for Sir Leslie and the entire family. He came to rely entirely on his daughters. The problem of caring for the self-pitying tyrant fell first to Stella Duckworth, Sir Leslie's stepdaughter. After her marriage, she even consented to live in the house across the street so she could supervise her ailing stepfather. Unfortunately, she died only a few months later, and the task of caring for Sir Leslie passed to Vanessa. Sir Leslie's demands on his daughters increased, and by the time he died of cancer in 1904, the effects of stress and responsibility were so great that Virginia suffered her second breakdown.

Following the death of their father, the Stephen children moved to 46 Gordon Square in Bloomsbury. Thoby began inviting friends from his Cambridge University days to what would become regular Thursday night gatherings.

In 1906, Thoby, Vanessa, Virginia, and a friend named Violet Dickinson set off to visit Greece. They became ill from drinking unboiled milk, and Thoby contracted typhoid fever and died. Shortly after this tragedy, Vanessa married Clive Bell, one of Thoby's friends from Cambridge. Virginia moved to 29 Fitzroy Square with her brother Adrian, and the Thursday night meetings continued at this new address.

Many brilliant young men passed through Virginia and Adrian's salon. The Stephen sisters had gained a reputation for their intelligence and their beauty. Although Virginia hoped to marry someday, it's probable she feared the sexual nature of such a commitment. Some years before, her stepbrother George Duckworth had made overt sexual advances to the young and inexperienced Virginia. It has also been suggested that both George and his brother Gerald may have physically abused their stepsister, although exactly what happened is not known. Her terror undoubtedly contributed to the fear and disgust she would later express toward sex.

In 1911, Adrian and Virginia moved to Brunswick Square and divided up their house to accommodate boarders. The famous economist John Maynard Keynes and his lover Duncan Grant occupied the first floor. Virginia moved into rooms on the third floor, while Adrian lived on the second. Leonard Woolf, who was on leave from a civil service position in Ceylon, rented rooms on the fourth floor. Leonard was Jewish, very serious, and very persistent. As soon as he fell in love with Virginia, he began writing long and passionate letters. When Virginia accepted his proposal, she embarked upon a spiritual marriage that would sustain her all her life.

When Leonard Woolf married Virginia in 1912, he had little knowledge of her mental disease or of her sexual frigidity. A young man with a healthy amount of passion, Leonard may have assumed he could develop, through gentle understanding and love, his wife's sexual nature. If so, he was wrong. Although distressed by his own frustrating dilemma, Leonard became increasingly anxious about Virginia's mental condition. Almost one year after their marriage, Virginia took an overdose of Veronal and began for Leonard Woolf a thirty-year emotional roller coaster. On the advice of Virginia's doctors, Leonard decided to dismiss the possibility of having children. Throughout her life, Virginia regarded her lack of children as a kind of failure.

When Leonard met Virginia, she had begun seriously to pursue a writing career. She wrote reviews for the *Guardian* and the *Times Literary Supplement*. She was a perfectionist and rewrote her articles many times. She began her first novel, *The Voyage Out*, around 1907 and worked on it for six years. The novel was published in 1915.

In the years following her marriage, Virginia became increasingly prolific and wrote some of her greatest fiction. *Night and Day*, one of her few attempts at a traditional novel, was published in 1919. Later she embarked upon new themes and more experimental uses of language. Published in 1922, *Jacob's Room* employs the technique known as "stream of consciousness." The book contains no definite plot. Rather than using action to advance the story, stream of consciousness relies on impressions of thought and feeling, not always related. Through language, Woolf creates a poetic portrait of youth.

Originally called "The Hours," *Mrs. Dalloway* (1925) resounds with the chimes of Parliament's Big Ben signaling the passage of time. Set amid the clamor and energy of London, the story takes place during one day in the life of Clarissa Dalloway.

To the Lighthouse (1927) marks the culmination of Virginia Woolf's "vision," as many scholars have termed her innovative use of language and character. *To the Lighthouse* is built on a structure of three sections representing three different periods of time. Although the main character is Mrs. Ramsey (who many critics believe is based on Virginia's mother), the primary voice is that of Lily Briscoe, an artist. She, like Virginia, realizes her own vision of life. The sea plays a central role in the story, demonstrating an inherent tranquility and beauty while symbolizing life's insignificance and transitory nature.

Woolf was a master of description and vivid imagery. Her characters are very real, and yet their world is often dreamlike as they move between the past and the present. Virginia Woolf perfectly combined thoughts with visual impressions. She probed her own imagination while drifting through the minds of a tapestry of characters. Her unique writing style was well received by the public, and her reputation grew as she became one of the most widely read novelists of her day.

In addition to their various writing projects, Leonard and Virginia decided to take up printing. They bought a hand-press and began printing small books and pamphlets. Soon, what had begun as a therapeutic pastime evolved into a small, yet highly respected publishing house. The Hogarth Press published works by E.M. Forster, Katherine Mansfield, and T.S. Eliot, as well as the translated writings of Sigmund Freud.

As Virginia attained a certain degree of celebrity, many people passed in and out of her life. None would influence her more than Vita Sackville-West. Vita was a beautiful woman with striking features inherited from her Spanish and aristocratic English lineage. She had been raised at Knole, one of England's largest and most famous ancestral homes. Both she and her husband, Harold Nicolson, were bisexual. A poet and novelist herself, Vita admired the famous older writer, and eventually they formed an intense attachment sustained primarily through passionate words and letters. Virginia based her great fantasy "biography" *Orlando* (1928) on the life of Vita. This aristocratic, four-hundred-year-old character changes from a man to a woman in the course of the book. While chronicling the story of Orlando, Virginia also traced the history of English literature. The book is dedicated to Vita.

While Virginia's relationship with Vita may have furthered her feminist beliefs, Virginia had become aware of the inequality of the sexes in both society and the arts at an early age. She outlined her thoughts on women and fiction in her brilliant essay *A Room of One's Own* in 1929. This essay discusses women's exclusion from the history of literature and explores the sacrifice and dedication necessary for the creation of art.

Her next book, *The Waves* (1931), signaled the beginning of a decline in Virginia's emotional stability. This "poem-play," as she called it, represented a further shift in her literary style. By the time she had edited and re-edited the proofs, her anxiety and the resulting headaches had returned. In *The Waves,* three male and three female characters symbolize the cycle of life. Their words are filled with images of nature, day and night, life and death. In this work, Woolf explores the dreams, hopes, accomplishments, and disappointments of her characters by using an experimental framework of form and language.

Although she feared the onset of a breakdown, she nevertheless continued to write. In 1933, she published *Flush,* a delightful biography of Elizabeth Barrett Browning's spaniel. In 1937, *The Years* was published, followed by *Three Guineas* in 1938. The feminist ideas expressed in *Three Guineas* were even more radical than those in *A Room of One's Own.*

While she was working on her last novel, *Between the Acts* (published after her death in 1941), several very real and frightening events began to overshadow Virginia's world. Her nephew Julian was killed in the Spanish Civil War, and all of England was growing nervous about the threat posed by Adolf Hitler. In the event the Nazis invaded England, Leonard and Virginia agreed to take poison rather than see Leonard taken away to a concentration camp.

In 1941, the sky above England was filled with the sound of fighter planes and artillery fire. With such dark possibilities before her, it is not surprising that the dreaded voices began to invade her mind again.

On March 28, 1941, she wrote letters to Vanessa and Leonard, walked to the banks of the River Ouse, and drowned. Although she wrote and spoke about the dark reality of death, Virginia Woolf also celebrated her artistic gifts and recognized the joyous aspects of life. In *To the Lighthouse,* she eloquently described what was perhaps her perception of existence:

> What is the meaning of life? That was all—a simple question; one that tended to close in on one with years. The great revelation had never come. The great revelation perhaps never did come. Instead there were little daily miracles, illuminations, matches struck unexpectedly in the dark.

Anne Frank

Anne Frank

I want to write, but more than that, I want to bring out all kinds of things that lie buried deep in my heart.

Anne Frank's *The Diary of a Young Girl* is a profound testament to life itself. The diary is poignant evidence that even in the face of unimaginable suffering, the human spirit can be courageous, optimistic, imaginative, and full of hope.

Anne Frank had a great love of life and a strong desire to learn about history, music, and literature. She wanted to travel, have a career, and fall in love. It is an unthinkable tragedy that she was denied these basic rights. *The Diary of a Young Girl* illustrates that individuals, and not masses, are the innocent victims of war. The diary shows the enormous potential that was wasted by the Nazis. Anne Frank represents the millions of young voices that were silenced in the concentration camps.

Anne Frank wanted desperately to live. She had learned to find joy in such small pleasures as looking at the sky, eating a bowl of strawberries, taking a bath, and writing in her diary. Her capacity for finding happiness in the depressing and claustrophobic "secret annex" underscores the fact that had she survived, Anne would have experienced life to the fullest and taken advantage of every opportunity.

In addition to having the normal hopes and dreams of a young girl, Anne Frank longed to become a writer. In contrast to all the things that were ultimately denied her, it is ironic that she did in fact achieve this goal. Although she was unable to realize the extent of her talent, Anne's diary afforded her the satisfaction of knowing she could write. In the privacy of her tiny niche, and unaware of the horrors she would someday face, Anne confessed her secrets to her diary. How could she have known that the outpourings of her heart would someday be read by millions of people in hundreds of languages throughout the world? "I want to go on living even after my death," she wrote.

The diary is a fascinating study in human psychology and a revealing look at why people write. Once an individual discovers this mode of expression, it's difficult to suppress the desire to create. Anne's love of words and of storytelling speaks in an incredibly powerful voice on every page.

Anne Frank was born on June 12, 1929, in Frankfurt, Germany. Although Anne's parents came from very wealthy Jewish families, their fortunes were lost in the financial collapse of Germany after World War I. Anne's father was a hardworking businessman, however, and he provided a comfortable life for his wife and two children. In 1933, Mr. Frank began to fear that Germany was no longer safe for Jews. He anticipated the persecution that was soon to follow, and he moved his family to Amsterdam, Holland. Holland had a history of providing sanctuary for people under persecution. However, the Nazis penetrated the Dutch borders, and Jews were once again in danger.

After the German invasion, life in Holland changed dramatically for its Jewish citizens. They were forced to wear large yellow stars on their clothing. They couldn't attend the theater, ride on public transportation, or visit Christian families. They had a strict curfew and could only shop in restricted stores. Anne was forced to leave the Montessori School and attend a Jewish school.

Although Mr. Frank tried to maintain a normal life, he and most Jewish adults were aware of the growing threat to their safety. The Germans had begun to deport Jews to concentration camps. In July of 1942, Mr. Frank warned Anne that her life might change very quickly. He encouraged her to enjoy her youthful pursuits for as long as possible.

When Anne's sixteen-year-old sister Margot unexpectedly received a notice from the German police, Mr. Frank told the family to gather together their most precious belongings. Rather than arouse suspicion by carrying suitcases, the Franks each put on several layers of sweaters, skirts, and pants and left their home forever.

Although the Germans had forced Mr. Frank to leave his business, his non-Jewish colleagues arranged to hide the Frank family in several rooms at the back of the office building. Anne was unaware that her father and mother had been storing supplies for many months. The Franks were joined in the "secret annex" by a business associate, Mr. Van Daan. His wife, their son, Peter, and a dentist named Albert Dussel also joined the group.

The unusual conditions made life difficult for everyone. Because the building was occupied during the day, the Franks and the other residents of the annex had to remain absolutely quiet. Heavy curtains covered the windows, and no one could run water, walk, talk, or even sneeze. The building was empty in the evenings and on weekends, but the Franks were still afraid a plumber, charwoman, or neighbor might see them and notify the Gestapo.

Their loyal friends in the building brought food, clothing, and gifts for the hideout. There were few pleasures, and circumstances were so oppressive that everyone bickered and started petty arguments.

Anne's diary was her only means of escape. The diary had been a gift for her thirteenth birthday. Less than four weeks later, it was one of the few possessions she took into hiding. Anne regarded her diary as the close friend she'd always longed for. She named it "Kitty" and wrote each entry as if it were a letter. She began, "Dear Kitty" and ended, "Yours Anne."

The time spent with her "friend" quickly became the highlight of her days. She shared many details of life in the annex. She longed for a better relationship with her mother, and she wrote of the great love she felt for her father. She also described how her innocent flirtation with Peter Van Daan developed into a tender romance between two young people craving love and fantasy.

When she wrote, only infrequently, about war or politics, she conveyed the overwhelming terror that was always present. But otherwise Anne's words are those of an exceptionally bright, happy teenager. She was extremely honest in describing her attributes and faults. She was so positive, idealistic, and forgiving that as one approaches the final pages, it becomes hard to believe that this doomed young girl had less than one year to live.

In addition to her diary, Anne also wrote short stories. They have been published, and are widely read throughout the world. Anne wanted to become a professional journalist. She wanted a different life from that of her mother and Mrs. Van Daan, and vowed not to waste her time with idle domesticity. She wanted to work toward an ideal.

The members of the secret annex experienced several close calls during their last months of hiding. Because of the food shortage and lack of employment in Holland, hungry people began breaking into homes and offices. Each time burglars broke into their building, the Franks were afraid the police would arrest them instead of the thieves.

On August 4, 1944, the secret annex was discovered and the members were sent to concentration camps. It was the first time

Anne had been outside in over two years. For a very small sum of money, an employee of the building had turned the Franks, the Van Daans, and Mr. Dussel over to the Gestapo. Mr. Frank was the only member of the group to survive the war.

After she was taken from the annex, Anne was first sent to Auschwitz and was later moved to Bergen-Belsen. She became ill and died before her sixteenth birthday.

A visit to the secret annex on the Prinsengracht Canal in Amsterdam is an experience few visitors can forget. The building is a museum and memorial to Anne Frank. Her movie star pictures and postcards still hang on the wall, and one can imagine Anne crouched in a corner, writing in the precious diary that was found after her arrest.

When the train pulled up at Auschwitz, Anne undoubtedly feared she would never write again. She may have wondered who, if anyone, would read or care about her words:

> I can shake off everything if I write; my sorrows disappear, my courage is reborn. But, and that is the great question, will I ever be able to write anything great, will I ever become a journalist or a writer? I hope so, oh, I hope so very much, for I can recapture everything when I write, my thoughts, my ideals and my fantasies... So I go on again with fresh courage; I think I shall succeed, because I want to write!

Agatha Christie

Agatha Christie

Whenever Agatha Christie filled out an application form, she wrote "married woman" on the line marked "occupation." She was reluctant to put "writer," even after she'd written several books and become quite well established. Christie always found it hard to distinguish between writing as a hobby and writing as a career. Perhaps she felt this conflict because writing came easily to her or because in her early years she had pursued her craft on the sly. Whatever the reason, Christie hesitated to admit that she was, in her words, "a bona fide author."

It seems highly ironic that these feelings should come from a writer who achieved such staggering success. Agatha Christie was amazingly prolific, and her books rank among the top bestsellers of all time. She wrote sixty-seven novels and sixteen collections of short stories. Her play *The Mousetrap* has had one of the longest runs in theater history. Although she wrote mysteries with intricate and clever plots, one doesn't need a detective to discover why she wrote so well and so often. She loved planning a story and solving the crime.

Agatha Mary Clarissa Miller was born on September 15, 1890, in Torquay, on the coast of England. Her father, Frederick, was an American. He was forty-four when Agatha was born. Her mother, Clara, was thirty-six. Agatha, the youngest of three children, was raised in a large house with an abundance of servants. She always spoke lovingly of her childhood and carried happy memories of it throughout her life.

Her mother wrote poetry and instilled in her children a love of books and reading. Clara Miller did not believe in sending her children to school, so Agatha was educated at home. Agatha remembered how quickly her life changed after her father died. Even though she was only eleven, she marked the sad occasion as the end of her childhood.

Although she also wrote poetry as a young woman, Agatha's true aspiration was to become a concert pianist. When she was told she lacked the "temperament" to play, she briefly considered a singing career as an alternative.

Agatha became aware of her literary calling when she was eighteen and confined to bed with influenza. Her mother sensed her boredom and suggested she write a story to pass the time. Agatha's older sister, Madge, had experienced some success selling short pieces to *Vanity Fair.* Agatha was evidently inspired by her initial attempt, and she finished a six-thousand-word story entitled "The House of Beauty." She typed the words in purple ink on her sister's old typewriter. She signed the story "Mac Miller, Esq."

Agatha's fascination with the occult is evident even in this early piece. Stories by Edgar Allan Poe were popular at this time, and a curiosity about mysticism and spiritualism can be seen in this story and in the plots of many of Agatha's later works.

Even though "The House of Beauty" was rejected by several magazines, Agatha continued to write stories. She also completed a novel. On the advice of a neighbor, she submitted the novel to a publisher. Unfortunately, it was also rejected.

Agatha temporarily put her writing on hold during her courtship with Archibald Christie. He was a member of the Royal Flying Corps, and in the early 1900s this carried with it a great deal of romance and glamour. They were married on Christmas Eve, 1914, after a two-year engagement. During

World War I, Archie was sent away for a six-month tour of duty in the Corps. It was during this time that Agatha studied to become a pharmacist.

Agatha and her sister Madge had become very close over the years. As both young women were writers, they were constantly encouraging one another to tackle new and challenging subjects. Once, while they were discussing a favorite detective novel, Madge dared her sister to write one. Although she didn't begin right away, Agatha made up her mind she would prove to Madge she could indeed write such a story.

It was while she was working in the pharmacy that Agatha remembered her promise. Her job allowed her a few free hours every day, and she decided to use them for writing. Surrounded by bottles of poison, she decided quickly how the poor victim would meet his or her death. She next went in search of her characters. It was for this first novel that Agatha created Hercule Poirot, the Belgian detective. She worked diligently, and even locked herself in a hotel room for two weeks until she'd finished the book.

The Mysterious Affair at Styles was rejected by four publishers. In one final attempt at publication, Christie sent the manuscript to John Lane at The Bodley Head publishing house and then forgot about it. Archie came home from the war to work in the Air Ministry Office in London. Soon after his return, Agatha learned she was pregnant. On August 5, 1917, Rosalind was born. Two years later Agatha heard from John Lane. The Bodley Head had accepted her manuscript.

Agatha Christie once made this comment about writing: "The most blessed thing about being an author is that you do it in private and in your own time." The craft of writing perfectly suited Christie's life-style and personality. She was always aware that money was an important result of writing. She knew a magazine story would pay a certain amount and that she could receive even greater earnings from a book. When she needed money to save her family home, Archie suggested she write another book.

There are many reasons why Agatha Christie became a complete master of the detective novel. Early on, she learned what type of writing best suited her talents, and she decided not to stray too far off course. Christie was always fascinated by the battle between good and evil, and she was intrigued by the ways in which passion could make ordinary people commit truly extraordinary crimes.

From her first novel to her last, she seldom varied her method of writing. She decided on a crime and then worked out such details as who, what, when, where, and why the dastardly deed had occurred. She believed in pulling the unexpected from ordinary situations. Christie did not believe in depending too closely on real people for characters. She once described how she sat on a tram and picked out interesting bits from the men and women seated nearby. She then compiled these ingredients into her fictional characters. Christie once referred to the writing process as a "chore." The plots came easily, but the execution was often laborious. She was very disciplined, however, and sometimes produced two or three books a year.

Although Christie never deliberately sought publicity, a famous incident focused the spotlight on her personal life. When Archie confessed he was in love with another woman and wanted a divorce, Christie went into a state of temporary shock and disappeared for eleven days. The newspapers learned of the story and turned it into a sensational scandal. When she reappeared, claiming a loss of memory, Christie had become more famous than ever. The "disappearance" was always a painful subject for Christie. Many members of the press believed the entire incident had been a hoax or a publicity stunt.

After her divorce, Christie continued writing detective novels and also published several nondetective novels under the pseudonym Mary Westmacott. In 1929, she met an archeologist named Max Mallowan whom she later married. He was fifteen years her junior.

Agatha Christie lived the ideal life of a writer. The richness of her plots was complemented by the fullness of her real life. Writing was a source of great pleasure for Christie. She always regarded her success and subsequent wealth as an unexpected bonus. In 1971, she was made Dame Commander in the Order of the British Empire. "What can I say at seventy-five?" asks Christie in the last line of her autobiography. "Thank God for my good life."

Lorraine Hansberry

Lorraine Hansberry

Lorraine Vivian Hansberry's early death ended the promise of a brilliant career. She died of cancer at the age of thirty-four. Hansberry was the first black woman to have a play produced on Broadway. She was also the youngest person and the first black dramatist to win the New York Drama Critics' Circle Award for the Best Play of the Year. Her prize-winning work, *A Raisin in the Sun,* is set in Chicago.

Hansberry was born in Chicago on May 19, 1930. When she was eight, her parents moved into a wealthy all-white neighborhood. Her memories of being hit, cursed, and spat upon there would last all her life. When the family was evicted, Lorraine's father and the NAACP took the case before the Supreme Court and won a landmark decision. Hansberry always believed her father's early death was a result of the emotional suffering he experienced because of this case.

Although Hansberry briefly attended the University of Wisconsin, she left after two years. She hoped to receive a more useful education through some type of employment. She went to work as a journalist on the black paper *Freedom.* The paper's editorial board was chaired by Paul Robeson. The job enabled Hansberry to meet other writers such as W.E.B. Du Bois and Langston Hughes. It was during the course of this work that Hansberry made the decision to become a writer. While still in college, she had accidentally observed a rehearsal of Sean O'Casey's *Juno and the Paycock.* She remembered the impact the words of the Irish people made upon her, and she hoped to one day infuse her writing with the same passion O'Casey gave to his characters. "One of the most sound ideas in dramatic writing," she explained, "is that in order to create the universal, you must pay very great attention to the specific." In her plays, Hansberry attempted to take human suffering beyond the black experience and apply the lessons to people of all races.

A Raisin in the Sun is about the American dream and the effect materialistic values have on a poor black family. The characters believe money can not only solve their personal problems, but can alleviate some of the suffering they experience as blacks. When the family receives an unexpected $10,000, each member fantasizes about the miraculous changes the money can and will bring. The money is lost to a con man, and the play ultimately shows that no matter how great the loss, a person can still maintain his or her integrity.

A Raisin in the Sun went on to become a movie (for which Hansberry wrote the screenplay) and a musical entitled *Raisin.* The play was translated into thirty languages and was produced in many countries, including Mongolia, Kenya, the Soviet Union, and Czechoslovakia.

Hansberry's cancer had already been diagnosed when her next play, *The Sign in Sidney Brustein's Window,* was produced on Broadway. She was forced to attend many rehearsals in a wheelchair. It was not as well received as her previous play, and it closed, after 101 performances, on the night of Hansberry's death. The play focuses on several artists and intellectuals living in Greenwich Village. As if to underscore her theme of universality, the play contains only one black character, Alton Scales, a political activist. The play also became famous when Hansberry's dedicated admirers made a passionate appeal to keep the show running. One woman donated her entire savings of $8,500, and many prominent people made substantial contributions. At the "final" performance, another $5,000 was collected; the play continued for an additional week.

During a march against discrimination at New York University, Hansberry had met a young songwriter and musician named Robert Nemiroff. They were married in 1953. Although they divorced shortly before her death, Nemiroff became her literary executor, editing most of her work that appeared after 1965.

On the second anniversary of her death, the New York radio station WBAI asked Nemiroff to compile portions of Hansberry's work for a tribute. The result was "To Be Young, Gifted and Black." The original program was seven and a half hours long, and its cast included Sidney Poitier and Bette Davis. It was from this radio tribute that the Off-Broadway production evolved. The biographical piece used scenes from Hansberry's plays as well as excerpts from her letters and journals. The play toured the country and was presented on hundreds of college campuses.

Three additional plays were published in a posthumous volume in 1972. These works illustrate Hansberry's concern with such international issues as the development of nuclear weapons. She also wrote about Africa and black Americans' search for their African heritage. She began *Les Blancs* in 1960 and worked on it until her death. Nemiroff adapted the final version, which appeared on Broadway in 1970. In the play, the character Tshembe Matoseh returns to Africa and becomes involved in a violent revolution. Hansberry was a devoted student of African history. Her uncle, William Leo Hansberry, was a prominent African scholar. She read a great deal about African culture and studied African history under W.E.B. Du Bois.

Her two other plays, *The Drinking Gourd* and *What Use Are Flowers?*, have never been produced in their entirety. Portions have been staged in the biographical piece "To Be Young, Gifted and Black."

In addition to her concerns about black issues and nuclear war, Hansberry considered herself a feminist and regarded Simone de Beauvoir's *The Second Sex* as "the most important book in America." In her ironically titled essay "In Defense of the Equality of Men," Hansberry argues that women are wrongly blamed for the changes brought about by so-called feminism. She argues that all societies evolve and that change is inevitable. By breaking traditions and analyzing the impact of male and female conditioning, both sexes can only gain from the reevaluation of their roles.

Hansberry wrote over sixty newspaper and magazine articles as well as poems, plays, and speeches. She juxtaposed her ideas on racial equality with a sensitivity and compassion for all people. She aspired to better the human condition, and people of all races were deprived of a sympathetic voice when she died on January 12, 1965.

4

Contemporary Authors

The following interviews provide a revealing look into the lives of twelve working writers. Each writer's journey toward success has been different, and yet they all seem to concur in the belief that writing involves a total commitment of body, mind, and soul. While the demands of their careers are very intense, writing also provides them enormous gratification. Writing forms the core of their natures, around which everything else in their lives revolves. Some of these writers are reclusive, while others are very visible, perhaps tracking down a story, publicizing a forthcoming work, or teaching. The importance of education is a dominant theme throughout these interviews. The authors appear unanimous in voicing this advice for aspiring writers: "Read, read, read!"

These writers did not achieve their goals through any extraordinary amount of luck, but rather through hard work and determination to succeed in their profession. Each writer speaks with candor about her unique experience of personal as well as professional accomplishments and disappointments. The writers share a love of words and a fascination with the process involved in telling a real or imaginary story.

These writers also share a certain courage that enables them not only to write, but to live with a sense of awareness and conviction. Perhaps the bond that links the writers of the past with these contemporary authors is artistic courage. "Be a risk taker," advises the journalist Jan Goodwin. A writer takes many risks with her ideas, and she must also face an ongoing inner challenge.

If one were to pull a common theme from these interviews, it would be the writers' ability to overcome the struggle between dreaming and doing. As the novelist Carolyn See explains, "If you hook up with that courage, give yourself a focus, and add ambition, you're in business." These writers have all learned how to push, to test again, to fail, to push harder, and to succeed. Without courage, their manuscripts would have remained reams of empty pages.

In the following interviews, five novelists, two poets, one newspaper journalist, one playwright, one screenwriter, one young adult novelist, and one magazine journalist offer their unique perspectives on a writer's life.

Dawn Garcia

Dawn Garcia

Dawn Garcia is a reporter for the *San Francisco Chronicle*. After only one month on the job, her editor asked her to cover the 1986 earthquake in El Salvador. She was one of two reporters on the *Chronicle* who spoke fluent Spanish. In less than twenty-four hours, Dawn was on the plane. Now her "beat" is City Hall.

Raised in Cupertino, California, Dawn Garcia is a graduate of Cupertino High School and the University of Oregon's Department of Journalism. She is married to a free-lance photojournalist.

Why do you write?
DG: I enjoy the challenge. It's as scary as it is exciting to try and translate an experience or an event into words that lie flat on the paper. You really want to share the experience with the readers, and you hope your words will allow them to feel the same things you did.

When did you decide to become a newspaper reporter?
DG: I didn't really get into newspaper writing until I was in college. I took a lot of English classes in high school, and I thought I might be an English major in college. I was always the person who liked to answer essay questions. In college, someone suggested I try working for the student paper because they

knew I liked to write. I've always kept journals. I've got tons of them from years ago. It's fun to go back and reread them. Anyway, I always wanted to be a writer, and I always did a great deal of reading. I think the two go hand in hand. I started out as a reporter on the college newspaper and then became city editor. It was a very small paper and there were only five reporters altogether. This experience was the one that sparked my interest in newspapers.

How did you get your job on the Chronicle?
DG: The *Chronicle* is the third paper I've worked on. Working for several different papers is fairly typical of most reporters' careers. I've moved up somewhat faster than many people, and this is the result of a little bit of luck and a lot of hard work. Right before I graduated from college, I did an internship at the *Oregon Journal,* an afternoon paper that later merged with the *Oregonian,* a morning paper. The *Oregonian* is Oregon's major paper. I would suggest an internship or something of that nature for anyone who wants to work on a paper. As an intern, you're like an apprentice reporter, and you really get a chance to see whether you enjoy this type of work. After my internship, I worked on a paper in Oceanside, near San Diego. I worked there for almost a year and a half. I then went to Modesto, California, and worked on the *Modesto Bee.* I covered City Hall and the courts there. When I decided to return to the Bay Area, I applied to several different papers. Fortunately, I was able to convince the people at the *Chronicle* to hire me.

Was it difficult getting the job?
DG: Yes, it was. I'm one of the youngest reporters at the *Chronicle.* I don't really know what the job situation is right now, but when you're looking for work, it helps to be energetic. Additionally, you really need to pay your dues. That's part of it.

A lot of people would like to start at the *Chronicle* right away, and yet very few people can just walk right in and become a reporter.

Describe your writing style.
DG: Newspaper writing is different from other types of writing. You write every day, and consequently it's possible to fall into certain ruts. Because newspaper writing can become so routine, it's important to have two different kinds of skills. You need to write succinctly, and you also need to write quickly and really pound something out if you have to. At the same time, however, you want to try and express real feelings and a sense of atmosphere about whatever it is you're covering.

What is your average deadline?
DG: One day. The deadline is also determined by how much time you have to write the story. For example, I got wind that something was going on at City Hall today, but I really didn't know for certain I'd have a story until around 4:30. That left me about an hour to write.

What is the difference between an investigative reporter and a beat reporter?
DG: A beat reporter generally writes a lot more stories. You "turn" a story daily. You gather all the information very quickly, and then you write the story. I find the excitement very satisfying. I try not only to make the deadline, but to make the story "sing." I also complement these regular stories with occasional projects that are longer. I'll work on these projects while I'm writing my daily stories. The term "investigative reporter" tends to refer to people who work for months on long research projects. But in fact, every reporter investigates stories every day, so the term could be universally applied.

What is the average length of the stories you write every day?
DG: We write in inches, and it's difficult to translate inches into an exact word count. It winds up being anywhere from one to five double-spaced typewritten pages. You tend to get a feeling for how long the story will be when you ask yourself, "What's the story worth?" Sometimes space is tight and you have no choice. Space is determined by how much advertising will appear in the paper. It's easy to write long stories and a lot harder to keep them tight.

Do you use "who, what, when, where, why, and how" or another method when you're tracking down a story?
DG: I think you need to get all that information into the story, but sometimes you need even more. The most challenging aspect of writing for a newspaper is that you're able to tell people what happened, give the basic five W's, and then try to put the reader exactly where you were. I just did a story about our new mayor. I convinced him I wanted to be in his home while he and his family were getting ready for the inauguration. I enjoy doing the kind of stories that take the reader beyond the headlines.

Do you have any choice about what you write?
DG: It's about half and half. As a beat reporter, you have more choice within a certain realm. Because you're there all the time and the editor isn't, you're able to know your area better than anyone else. Although the editors trust my judgment, they also add their input and ideas.

Was it difficult learning to meet daily deadlines?
DG: Yes, especially at the beginning. A reporter must learn to concentrate on what doesn't go into the story as well as what goes in. If you've reported a story correctly, you'll always end up

with all kinds of information you can't use. That's the hardest part of trying to pace yourself. I think most people at the beginning, including myself, tend to go out and report and report and report. Consequently, you don't always leave yourself enough time to write. If you don't have enough time, your stories are probably not as good as they could be. You need to budget your time for reporting as well as for fine tuning and reworking your material.

Are you as disciplined and organized in other areas of your life?
DG: I believe I'm a pretty organized person.

What other traits do you possess that make your personality well suited to being a reporter?
DG: I am aggressive and assertive, and I suppose I've become even more so since I became a reporter. I've always been outgoing and I've always enjoyed talking with people. That's one of the things about being a reporter. You certainly can't be reclusive. When you're working a beat like City Hall, you have to meet and befriend a lot of people. You have to make friends with people because you may need their help later on. If you just come up and say, "I need this or that," you're not going to get anywhere.

Isn't it also true that you can't be intimidated by someone like the mayor?
DG: Yes, that's one of the most important things. You also can't take no for an answer. You need to be very persistent.

Are you sensitive about people's feelings when you go after a story?
DG: Very much so. I think one of the biggest myths about reporters is that they're insensitive, and that they love running

up to people whose children have just died in a plane crash and saying, "How do you feel?" The public doesn't understand that as reporters, we treat private people differently from public figures. Private citizens have the right to their privacy. Public figures open themselves up to public scrutiny, and that's very different.

Would you ever say no to your editor if you were assigned a story that didn't go along with your beliefs?
DG: Yes. Although I don't think I've ever been asked to do something I really didn't feel right about, I would say no if that were the case. I find it interesting that grieving families often consider it helpful to talk with reporters. These people sometimes need to talk with someone objective. We can be very good ears.

What do you do if they tell you something that will enhance your story but you know they didn't intend to say?
DG: That's a matter of judgment. My position is that public figures know, when a reporter calls, they can expect to be quoted. I make it very clear when I interview someone who is not accustomed to talking to reporters. I tell them I'm a reporter and that I'm writing a story. If they don't want to be quoted, I ask them to tell me. We set the ground rules right away.

Does the pressure get to you?
DG: At times. I do have to push myself and not let the pressure get to me. I've only had the City Hall beat for five months. Before that I was what they call a "general assignment reporter." That really means writing about a little bit of everything. At City Hall, I work in a small press room and a reporter from the competing paper sits in the same room. Sometimes that person

can hear what I'm saying, and vice versa. It can become very competitive. I wish I didn't take my work home as often as I do. Sometimes I'll even have dreams about stories that I'm working on.

I think part of the writing process is unconscious. Some of the writing is going on in your head, and ideas are gelling somewhere in the back of your mind. Therefore, when you sit down to write, you've already done some of the ground work. This process helps when I'm writing my leads. This is what we call the beginning of a story. It's the most important part because with your lead, you'll either pull readers in and they'll continue with the story, or they'll get bored and turn the page. Newspapers are different from books. When people read a book, they bear with the writer for a few pages. In newspapers, you only have a paragraph or two to pull them in. If the lead doesn't jump out at you when you're writing, you mull it around in your mind almost unconsciously. After thinking and dreaming about it, the lead will often pop out when you sit down to write.

Here it is 8:15 in the evening and you're still on the job. How does your work affect your marriage?
DG: My husband is very supportive. I think it would be really hard on a couple with different backgrounds. Because my husband is a photojournalist, he understands the demands of my schedule. It would be hard if he had a nine-to-five job. When I went to El Salvador, someone said to him, "I can't believe you let her go." And he replied, "What do you mean, I *let* her go? She's a big girl." He thought it was a great opportunity.

Do you want to have children?
DG: I hope children will figure in my future. Having children

is very hard for women reporters. There's not a lot of leeway for reporters to come back and work part-time. Everything will have to change because more and more women are becoming reporters, and it's certainly not the kind of job where you can count on being home at a certain time. Right now I'm a very career-oriented person, but I would like to have kids at some point.

What advice would you offer aspiring journalists?
DG: I think young people should not only perfect their writing skills, but they should read everything they can. They should become students of the world. I think there's a kind of movement right now among newspapers. Reporters are working very hard to make good writing a priority. We still have to get the news out, but it's also possible to make writing more literary. I've organized a group of reporters. We meet at my house and work on our writing. We've hired a writing coach, and we meet every other week and work on stories in progress or analyze past stories. We also bring in writing samples from other papers.

When you're considering a career in journalism, it's also great to be able to speak a second language. It's amazing that there are so few Spanish-speaking reporters in California. Newspapers are in dire need of reporters who speak other languages.

Do you consider yourself lucky to have the opportunity of working on a major newspaper?
DG: Yes. Many people would die to be working for the *Chronicle* or a paper of this size. I feel I have a front row seat on the world. I consider it a real privilege.

Does that inspire you to do your best?
DG: Yes. More than a million people read my paper every day. That's a responsibility. Sometimes I forget, but then I'll see a newspaper on someone's doorstep and think, "There it is. That person is reading my writing." When you're a reporter, people open themselves up and invite you into their lives.

Nikki Giovanni

Nikki Giovanni

Nikki Giovanni is a prolific poet and essayist. She began her literary career in the 1960s and became well known for her social and political activism. Her books include *Black Judgment; Black Feeling, Black Talk; Ego Tripping and Other Poems for Young Readers; The Women and the Men; Cotton Candy on a Rainy Day; Those Who Ride the Night Winds;* and her collection of essays *Gemini: an Extended Autobiographical Statement: My First Twenty-five Years of Being a Black Poet.* She is a popular speaker and has made several recordings of her poetry. Born in Knoxville, Tennessee, Nikki Giovanni has been awarded four honorary doctorate degrees.

Why do you write?
NG: It's what I do for a living. It's a talent and a craft. It's pleasurable. Writing is something I do as well as anything else. That doesn't make me a great American writer, but it does mean I bring a lot of joy and pride to my work.

Did you want to write when you were a young girl?
NG: I don't really believe in that concept. I don't believe people when they tell me they wanted to write as far back as kindergarten. I think most careers are evolutionary.

What attracted you to the craft of writing?
NG: It's the aspect of communication that makes writing so important. I also like to tell stories. I come from a big

storytelling family. I grew up just on the edge of television. My family would sit around on Sunday afternoons after church and tell stories and folktales. We shared information. We talked to one another. I like that aspect of writing.

Why did you become a poet? Did you ever want to be a novelist?
NG: I think the art form chooses the writer and not vice versa. I think poetically, not in images but in discontinuity. Poetry is uniquely qualified to put dissimilar information together to form a whole. You can start with a tangible and go to an intangible, or you can personify something abstract—it will all make a point. You can begin with words like "the leaves falling in my heart, darkness said to me: beware." You see, I've gone from a tangible to an intangible, personified an abstract, and made a point out of it. It's not a great poem yet, and I'd have to work on it, but it illustrates how these concepts work together. Poetry uses imagery and emotion to create something new. It's a process of blending the real and the unreal.

Do you think that explains why poetry can be so powerful?
NG: I don't just say this because I'm a poet, but I believe poetry is the heart of the language. Poetic images combine information and emotion in a way that no other medium can. Poetry enables you to get right to the heart of a subject. Poetry is powerful even when people don't understand all the images. T.S. Eliot's "The Waste Land" is one of my favorite poems. Even if you totally miss some of his references, you can still follow the poem on its emotion alone. That's what a poet does best. It's impossible to follow most other written mediums without information. Because of its rhythm, however, you can follow poetry. If you take any good, solid poem and read it, even though you may not understand all the language, the music of the words will carry the message.

You talk about the emotion of poetry. When you are seized by a passion, do you go right in and write it down?
NG: I'm seldom seized by passion. When people ask how I choose a subject, I like to use the word "interest." I become interested, or to some degree fascinated by a subject. As your interest grows, you begin to gather more and more information. Research is ninety percent of a writer's work. You attempt to discover what information can be brought to bear on the subject of your interest.

Do you jot things down and then put it all together?
NG: Some people might take that approach. I don't think I have a unique mind, but perhaps I have a different mind. I learned a long time ago that the things I cannot retain I should probably let go. It's just the way I think, and I don't necessarily recommend it. I teach a creative writing class, and I would not recommend this approach to my students. You try and make information your own. Learning is repetition, and you try and learn something over and over again until you no longer separate the subject from the information you've gathered. This is where your passion comes from. One of the things I stress to my students is that poetry cannot be the result of raw emotion. No matter how raw it may look, you must have information behind it, or it won't hold up. You might appreciate the idea, but nobody else will know what you're talking about.

Is this a lesson you've learned? Has your style changed over the years?
NG: I think I've made some stylistic changes. But the major change I see in my work is that I'm much more relaxed. I feel like the Kareem Abdul-Jabbar of poetry. The older I get, the more I understand how it's done. Right now I'm in a no-pressure zone. I think most people feel their writing life was

more or less an accident. You wonder how you got from point A to point B. Finally, you reach the point where you say, "I can write. I really know what I'm doing." After that, you can devote yourself to development.

Would you say that although it doesn't get any easier, you gain more confidence?
NG: There you go. We can learn a lot from athletes because they know the importance of practice. The more you write, and the more you practice your craft, the more relaxed you become.

Do you love writing as much as you always did?
NG: Everywhere I go, I recommend my profession. One thing is for certain, we'll never be flooded with writers. For example, if everyone that ever heard me speak took my advice and wrote a book, it would only enhance the human spirit. It could not detract from it. In many professions, there's an artificial restriction on the number of practitioners. In other words, we can have too many lawyers, doctors, and even librarians, but there will never be enough writers.

Don't you think we could also use more readers?
NG: Yes, we could use more readers. I do regret that Americans don't read as much as they once did. I think it's fair to point out that nothing conveys information better than a book, period. The information that is conveyed through television originally came from a book. If you really want to know what happened, you have to read about it in a book.

How can advanced education benefit the poet?
NG: I believe that poets are people, and what you want is an educated populace. In the same way that we're not going to have too many books, we're also not going to have too many

educated people. You want young writers and older writers as well to bring as much information as possible to their work. Experience is an important part of writing, and obviously, one cannot experience everything one writes about. One of the ways that writers allow themselves to experience things is through education. We can read about other people's lives. We can identify and internalize their experiences.

Do you think the criticism a poet receives in school can be dangerous to a fragile poet just discovering her voice?
NG: Everyone needs honest criticism, and part of that is going to be negative. If you're that fragile, you should be in another profession. Nobody would ever tell you that Robert Frost, Walt Whitman, or T.S. Eliot were fragile. And Anne Sexton, who was a tough, gutsy lady, wasn't fragile about her writing. She was fragile about life. I don't think we're fragile at all. I think we can handle criticism. Nothing galvanizes you better than someone saying you can't do it.

Your poetry was greatly affected by what was happening politically in the sixties. How do you think what's happening now will affect the poetry of young black women poets?
NG: I think there's been a lot of turning inward, and that's good. I think the black female is finding her voice and finding it is sufficient unto itself. If you go back to my generation, there was a compulsion to speak for a group of people because they were without a voice. And as we came through, for lack of a better word, the second emancipation, we freed people to speak for themselves and their own concerns. Today a Toni Morrison and a Ntozake Shange can write about what's interesting to them. They're not compelled to be the voice of a voiceless people.

Back in the sixties, your work expressed a lot of anger. Do you think there's as much anger today?
NG: I really don't know. Maybe there's anger, but right now, I think there's a lot of boredom out there. I embrace the boredom. I think it's real. It's the boredom of Alexander. In other words, the known world has been conquered. What excites me and keeps me interested is that the known world is not the end of the world. I'm interested in further exploration. All the nostalgia for the sixties is foolishness. It is an exercise in stupidity. I think that this too shall pass, and we'll realize we haven't even tapped our potential. People always say, "What should I do with my life?" Well, live it. Life is an existential situation. You live for the joy, and because you're a human being, you want to contribute to the common good. It's a constant search.

Do you see more possibilities in the world today than you did in the sixties?
NG: I wouldn't compare. I just wouldn't. We had a different situation and we've made it a little better. I'm proud of that, and I'm proud of whatever very small part I played. But we're quite some distance from human freedom, and that is my goal. This will not change overnight. I'm not a burnout. A lot of people from my generation got very disappointed because people didn't get up in the morning and say, "Now we're free." It had to be worked out. Human freedom is a continuing situation.

It seems today there's still so much to be angry about. Isn't the power of the poet timely right now?
NG: I would not be the right poet for that. We've opened up the doors; it's time to roll up our sleeves. Anger is pointless. It's right up there with guilt. So what? The question is, how are we going to utilize it? We have opportunity here. How are we going to take advantage of it?

What advice would you offer a young writer?
NG: Anyone who's thinking about becoming a writer must read. You'd be amazed at the number of young people who think they can write, and yet they don't read. I recently asked a class to name their favorite books and everyone blanked out. I said, "Okay, forget the plural. Name your favorite book. Well, how about any book you read recently?" And these are tomorrow's college students.

How would you suggest young people warm up to books?
NG: I don't recommend they warm up at all. I recommend they do it. Start with anything that's interesting, and when it becomes uninteresting, put it away. Some people think that if they begin a book, they have to finish it. Kids will buy a Michael Jackson album, but they don't listen to all of it at once. They listen to the songs they like and then they go back later and listen to the others. Books work the same way. You pick them up and use them as you need them. They are your friends.

Should poets write about all subjects or try to specialize?
NG: As a human being, you will find different things most important at different times in your life. My son just turned eighteen, so I have a teenage bias now. One day he'll probably have children, and I'll have a shifting interest as a grandparent. Between here and there I have my own life and the lives of people I love. I should be allowed to be funny when I feel funny and sad when I feel sad. I think our obligation as a species is to be Renaissance people. We shouldn't specialize. Writers are generalists.

Do you think you live twice as a writer?
NG: I don't think like that, but then I probably don't live in reality. My life is probably an illusion, and don't wake me up because I like it!

TOM ARMA, COURTESY E.P. DUTTON

Jan Goodwin

Jan Goodwin

Jan Goodwin has had a remarkable career in journalism. A native of England, Goodwin is a former executive editor of the *Ladies' Home Journal*. While at the *Journal*, she interviewed such public figures as Mother Teresa and Prime Minister Margaret Thatcher. She has covered wars and other volatile political situations in Afghanistan, El Salvador, Cambodia, and South Africa. Her best-selling book *Caught in the Crossfire* tells of the dangers she confronted disguised as a freedom-fighter in Afghanistan. Goodwin is currently working in Pakistan as program manager for the organization Save the Children.

Why did you become a writer?
JG: It was a happy accident. When I use that term, I really mean it. I was a math wiz. I was born in 1944, however, and in those days women didn't have the opportunity to become NASA space engineers. If you excelled in math, you had approximately two choices: I was offered the chance to become a teacher or a surveyor. No one said I could become a physicist or a space engineer. There were very few options. In addition to being a math wiz, I was a most voracious bookworm. Our home was filled with books.

How do you think the love of reading translates into the desire to write?

JG: Very early, you learn the power of the written word and the power to communicate. As a child, I was spellbound by all sorts of writers. I never set out specifically to become a journalist. When I got out of school, I just happened to have friends who were in journalism. But my first job was in publishing. I was an editorial assistant for an educational subsidiary of Doubleday. Then I started on a London weekly newspaper. The things that happened to me later were the result of a happy accident.

Why do you think you leaned toward journalism rather than writing fiction?
JG: I don't read a great deal of fiction. My personal taste is mostly nonfiction.

Is there one particular part of the writing process that you enjoy most?
JG: I really enjoy—in fact, I love—the reporting. I am a reporter. I love to report and research. I am one of those writers, and there are many of us, who do not enjoy the writing process. The writing process is exceedingly hard work. It's also a very scary process.

Why is it scary?
JG: I always procrastinate like mad. Before I started writing my book, I probably had the cleanest closets in town! Once you commit yourself to writing, you really put yourself on the line. Your work is out there for everyone to jump all over, and your ego is out there with it. I remember when I had to send the first four chapters of my book to the publisher. They wanted to see if I was on the right track. It happened to be my birthday. Afterward, I was paralyzed for a week. I couldn't move. I was on a very tight deadline, and I really couldn't afford to take

time out to wait for their reaction. My agent kept saying, "Don't be silly. They're going to take a while to get back to you." I knew I couldn't work until I heard what they said.

Even with all your experience, you were still scared?
JG: Yes. Even with all my experience. A lot of writers will identify with this fear.

Does it get better? Do you think it will be different for your next book?
JG: No, it probably won't be any different. Even though you write every day, it doesn't get any easier. Of course, there are times when the writing flows beautifully and you really think, "Great. This is wonderful!" You can look at one sentence and say to yourself, "This is pure *New Yorker*." The very next sentence you find yourself saying, "Is this typing, or is this writing?"

Does understanding the difficult process of writing make you less demanding as an editor?
JG: That's what all my writers used to ask! The answer is no. It really doesn't. I honor a deadline, and I get really mad when other people don't. I have dealt with writers in the past who have had a real horror of meeting deadlines. I can't tell you all the excuses I've heard. In order to get a story, I've even had a member of my staff sit with a writer who was blocked. I've heard the most ludicrous excuses. I've heard people say their briefcase with the manuscript was stolen or they got mugged. I don't have any patience for that type of thing. If you contract to do a job, you do it. I understand what writer's block feels like. The fact that I have been a writer and a reporter makes me understand the process. And for that reason, if someone does a

sloppy job, I get angry because I know it doesn't have to be done that way.

Why do writers get blocked? What causes it?
JG: Any shrink will tell you that the folks who have writer's block are perfectionists. They want so badly to be perfect, and yet they can never meet their own impossibly high standards. As a result, they never begin. The problem is, no one can ever be perfect.

How do you start? How do you just break through the writer's block?
JG: The only way to get through writer's block is to begin. It's the same as saying you're going to start a diet next Monday. If all you ever do is talk about it, you will never begin. The real discipline must come from within yourself. There are a lot of writers who receive an advance, and yet do not complete their book. They either give their advance back, or they get sued. There really is only one cure for writer's block, and that is to begin; even if it's not very good. Even if you throw it all out the window tomorrow—start writing. Once your fingers start going, your brain engages, and the pace picks up. You're moving. And once you're moving, the creative juices will get going too.

Do you think your desire to tell a story can overcome your fear of the situation you're forced to confront?
JG: Reporting often requires that you put yourself in a variety of situations. There are definite risks if you become involved in this profession. For example, I have been beaten up by an anarchistic group in England. When you go into a war zone, you do as much research as you can. You try to make the situation as safe as possible, trust the right people, and so on.

The rest, as they say, is in the hands of God. Obviously, you couldn't function in that kind of environment if you were petrified all the time.

What is the best part of being a journalist?
JG: One of the delights of journalism is that it's an ideal profession for a curious mind. I have traveled all over the world. I have met people from all walks of life, and I have seen all sorts of things. In the guise of journalism, you can ask virtually any question, of any person. I have never been bored. I feel sorry for people who get up in the morning and go to a job they loathe. In addition, journalism has definite advantages for women. You can step away for a while and have a family. It's not easy, but you can rock the crib with one hand and type with the other.

How do you overcome being intimidated by some of the people you interview?
JG: You will be intimidated at times. It can be a very intimidating experience to interview someone famous. But there are also times when the famous person is scared of you. It's always interesting when you realize this is what's going on. The best advice is to imagine the person you're interviewing doing something really mundane like brushing his or her teeth. Underneath the glamour of their position, they are, after all, very much like you.

How do you develop the confidence to interview someone like Margaret Thatcher? How do you prepare?
JG: You've used a very good word—prepare. Do your homework. Make sure you know your subject. Another thing I would advise a junior reporter is, don't cut off the person you're interviewing. I've read transcripts where someone's just about to say something interesting and the questioner asks another

question. The interviewer isn't listening to what's being said. She's gone in with a prepared list of questions. She hasn't listened to the way the interview is going. Instead, she just keeps firing like a machine gun. Listen to your subjects. Hear what they are saying. And, if you do your homework, you'll probably know when they're lying to you, when they're evading you, or whether they're giving you a stock interview. The two best tools of the reporter are: Number one, do your homework. Really know about the people you're interviewing. And number two, listen to what they're saying and what they're not saying. Don't rush to fill in the gaps.

What advice would you offer a young journalist who is just getting started?
JG: I am absolutely horrified when people tell me they want to be journalists and yet they have zero knowledge of current affairs. Don't tell me you want to be a journalist if you don't know or care to know anything about current affairs, to say nothing of geography. Read widely. It will help your writing style. Journalists become experts in a variety of fields. Even though they're somewhat superficial experts, they do become very knowledgeable. You have to have a curious mind to begin with, and you have to be interested in knowledge. If you don't read widely, you won't know the right questions to ask.

Do you have any additional advice?
JG: The most important advice is: Be ready to recognize and accept an opportunity. Most of us receive quite a lot of opportunities in life, and sometimes we are too nervous to accept them. Be a risk taker. Also, you must be willing to learn and be willing to work very hard. When I was a cub newspaper reporter, I can't tell you how many dates I was forced to stand

up at the theater because I couldn't reach them. I'd been sent off on assignment. Those kinds of things will happen. If you want to be a journalist, you're going to have to recognize that news is no respecter of nine-to-five hours.

Beth Henley

Beth Henley

Beth Henley was born in Jackson, Mississippi in 1952. Her best known play, *Crimes of the Heart*, won the Pulitzer Prize in 1981. The play also received a New York Drama Critics Circle Award, a Guggenheim Award, and a Tony nomination. Henley's screenplay adaptation of *Crimes of the Heart* was also nominated for an Academy Award. Her plays include *The Miss Firecracker Contest*, *The Wake of Jamey Foster*, *The Lucky Spot*, *Am I Blue*, and *The Debutante Ball*. Her screenplay credits include *True Stories* (with David Byrne) and *Nobody's Fool*. Henley is a graduate of Southern Methodist University.

Why do you write?
BH: You can pour your whole self into writing. It's engrossing. It gives you something to think about when you're standing in line at the grocery store, taking a shower, or driving your car. You don't have to worry about becoming bored. There's always something going on in your imagination.

Did you always want to be a writer?
BH: No. I wanted to when I was young, but when I started reading a lot of books, I thought writing might be too difficult.

What changed your mind?
BH: While I was in college studying acting, I took a course in

writing plays. I found I could write plays and dialogue. I'm not very good at writing narrative or anything like that.

Did you consciously decide not to pursue an acting career?
BH: I came to Los Angeles with the intention of trying to act, but I found it was very difficult. Writing is at least something you can do on your own.

How many plays did you write before Crimes of the Heart?
BH: I'd only written two one-act plays and a screenplay.

Were you aware that you might win the Pulitzer Prize?
BH: After *Crimes of the Heart* was produced at the Manhattan Theatre Club, the committee called to get my Social Security number. I asked them why, and they said, "We're nominating you for the Pulitzer Prize." I was really shocked. It was an honor even to be nominated. I didn't really think I would win.

How has your life changed as a writer?
BH: I have a better opportunity to have my plays produced. It's not as difficult getting people to read or look at my work.

Are people more apt to criticize your work?
BH: It's always a roll of the dice whether or not people are going to like what you've written. You just try and tell the story you want to tell. You're the one who has to work on it for two years, so you'd better write something you like. The public only has to look at it for two hours.

Do you get a lot of input about possible projects?
BH: A person isn't commissioned to write a play. You write it for yourself and then you try and sell it. It's different from writing movies. You're paid in advance for a movie and you

work for a studio or for a director or producer. With a play, however, you write it for yourself and hope someone will produce it.

Was it difficult to go from writing plays to writing movies?
BH: Writing movies is different. A writer doesn't really have that much control because the lines are often changed. I had a good rapport with the director of *Crimes of the Heart*. That's the most important thing when you're writing a movie. If the director doesn't share your vision, there's no way you can make the movie you want. I loved working with Bruce Beresford. He's directed several plays. I could feel his ideas and put them into my script. We had a lot of fun.

Do you keep a diary or a journal?
BH: I used to, but I've been pretty bad about it lately.

How do you get through hard periods in your life and work?
BH: When I get depressed, I sometimes write in a journal as a way of keeping track of just how depressed I am. This spring was the first time I got so depressed I couldn't work. I would basically sit with a pencil and a piece of paper for five minutes. Then I would try again for ten minutes and see if I could finally work up to half an hour and maybe write something.

Sometimes writers actually work better when they're melancholy. Do you find you're more productive when you're happy?
BH: I can't write when I'm too happy. I think I produce my best writing when my life is on some sort of even keel. I can get into a routine and a rhythm of work.

Do you write on a word processor?
BH: No. I write by hand in spiral notebooks.

Do you have any advice for young writers?
BH: I think the best advice I ever received is: Finish what you're working on. Start it and finish it. Don't worry about making each paragraph or each scene perfect. Just go ahead and plow through to the end. Once you're through, then you can go back and rework the scenes. You should even leave out the things you can't get right. People start projects and end up not liking what they've written. They start something else and leave that unfinished too. It's a bad pattern to get into.

Do you talk to yourself when you're writing dialogue?
BH: Yes, I think I do. I don't know if it's "out loud," but I definitely walk around my apartment thinking about the characters I'm working on.

Do you have any particular advice for aspiring playwrights?
BH: Read plays, go see plays, work on plays, and memorize speeches from plays. Learning to write is somewhat like osmosis. Structure and character somehow sink in. I'm convinced my acting experience helped me as a writer. I got to know each character separately and to think clearly as that person. I then transferred that ability to think clearly and specifically to all the characters, and I was able to know each character instead of just skimming the surface of all the other parts. You learn how to think specifically and you discover what works as an actor on stage. You know the type of dialogue you hate to get and the kind of work that's exciting to perform. I'd say yes, the more experience you have in the theater, the better.

How do you turn your own personal experience into fiction?
BH: I'm not really aware I'm writing about myself. I think about the story and about the characters that excite me. Of course the story always ends up being about something I've

experienced or wondered about subliminally. I always write about things that perplex me in my own life, things I haven't understood or grasped. I never write about things I understand. Of course, that would only make a short one-act. I write about things that cause me to ponder or to get angry.

Does writing about the dilemma help solve it?
BH: No, but I write about my own confusion. It's kind of like exorcism. Yet I'm often left with more questions than answers.

What do you want to be writing fifteen years down the road?
BH: I don't think about another Pulitzer Prize. I hope to continue writing about subjects that excite me. I also hope to make enough money so I don't have to work in any other type of job. I'm so blessed to be able to write about what interests me.

Do you have any advice about dealing with rejection?
BH: Having been an actor, I think the rejection one receives as a writer is much easier to take. At least they return your script on your doorstep. You don't have to be publicly humiliated. You have to be somewhat egotistical to sit down and think someone is going to read something you've written. You need a lot of self-esteem to be a writer. Of course that's mixed with complete insecurity. When you're working on a project, you have to be totally selfish and egotistical. Later, when you're sending it out and being rejected, that's something else altogether.

Do you believe that in order to succeed as a writer, you must have an overwhelming desire to write?
BH: Yes, and it's not even a question of will. It's not as though you have any choice. It's just what you have to do. You can't will yourself to write or not to write. You have to write whether you get paid or not. If you don't have to write, then don't.

Tama Janowitz

Tama Janowitz

Tama Janowitz published her first novel when she was twenty-three. A friend of Andy Warhol, she became well known in the media as a member of New York's literary and art scenes. A graduate of Barnard, Janowitz also has a Master of Fine Arts degree from Columbia University. She studied play-writing at Yale Drama School and creative writing at Hollins College. The recipient of two grants from the National Endowment for the Arts and a fellowship from Princeton University, Janowitz is the author of *American Dad, Slaves of New York,* and *A Cannibal in Manhattan.* She also wrote the screenplay for the movie made from her novel *Slaves of New York.*

Why are you a writer?
TJ: Although I've thought about that question, I really don't have an answer for it. Writing is what I do. It's my vocation. I can't really explain it.

Did your extensive education give you access to agents and other people in publishing?
TJ: No, but it gave me time to write. I wrote a novel while I was at Hollins College. I sent it out myself, and after it was returned a year later, I realized it was time to find an agent. I found one through the friend of a friend of somebody. The agent agreed to take me on, and then sold the book.

Why do you think you've become so successful? Is it because you're more visible than most writers?
TJ: I never felt I had to obey any rules. Generally speaking, if you want to be regarded as a serious writer, you're supposed to wear round glasses, have a braid, avoid doing any media, sit home, and be shy. *American Dad* sold a few copies but wasn't available in most bookstores. Even though it received some reviews, no one could ever find it to buy it. Five years went by between *American Dad* and the publication of my next book. During that time I wrote many books that no one wanted to publish. When *Slaves* was published by Crown, they said, "Would you be willing to do television, and would you be willing to make a literary video?" I said, "Absolutely," because it was the only way I could think to have people remember the name of the book or the name of the author. When someone goes into a bookstore and sees thousands of books, why does that person pick up a certain book? People only buy it if they've heard of it before. As a result of that thinking, I was willing to do everything, and consequently I received a lot of attention. Of course, you can't force people to write about you, but I let people know I was available and willing to be interviewed.

Do you think other writers are critical of you because you've decided not to hide?
TJ: I don't care whether they are or whether they're not. I've written the best I can and I'd like to sell the book. I don't really care what people think.

How did your connection with Andy Warhol help your career?
TJ: He was very emotionally supportive. We became friends after my stories began to appear in the *New Yorker*. He liked them very much and said he wished someone had been writing about the art world of the sixties in the way I was writing about the downtown art world of the eighties.

Do you enjoy writing, or is it hard for you?
TJ: It's very hard, and ninety percent of the time I dislike it intensely. I guess I wait for those moments when it's coming easily, or when I finish something and feel pleased for about five minutes.

How do you write?
TJ: I wait for the character to start speaking. That's when it gets exciting. I might throw out hundreds of pages while I'm waiting for the voice that's going to tell the story. Even though I might have an idea before, once the character begins talking in an authentic voice, that's when the story begins to be told. It may be different from the story I originally had in my head.

Do you have to be alone to hear that voice?
TJ: I try and get up in the morning and write. I need to be alone to write, but I also need to be around other people at least some of the time.

Are you very disciplined? Do you write between certain hours?
TJ: I write from around ten in the morning until one in the afternoon. That's about as much of that type of intense thinking as I can do at one time. If I am in the middle of a novel and it's going well, I often go back in the afternoon and revise what I've written in the morning.

Do you use a typewriter or word processor, or do you write in longhand?
TJ: I use a typewriter.

Do you have any superstitions connected with writing?
TJ: No. I don't like to talk about what I'm working on at the moment. Talking about it tends to dissipate the energy I have involved with the project.

How long did it take you to write A Cannibal in Manhattan?
TJ: It's very hard to say. It took several years. I had piles of notes and even drafts. *Cannibal* was finished in December of 1986. It's hard to say it took me from A to B. It was a total process.

Do you work well with editors? Are you receptive to criticism?
TJ: Yes, I am. I think you have to trust the person a great deal. That relationship often takes a while to develop. My editors at Crown have been fantastic. My editor at the *New Yorker* was wonderful. She's no longer there, but she was absolutely brilliant. Sometimes my mother reads my work and offers suggestions. She's a poet and a professor at Cornell.

Did you have an alternative plan if you didn't succeed as a writer?
TJ: I never really thought about it. Although it wasn't my first choice, my mother said I could live in her extra bedroom. I could never really think of anything else I wanted to do except write. That's another point. If people have too many things they're good at, it's easy to stop doing one thing and think you can move on to something else. In my case, however, I couldn't think of anything else to do.

Was it frustrating when your first book was published and your publisher wasn't promoting it in the stores?
TJ: I don't really think a person has any control over that. All you can do is say, "Well, they didn't publish the last book at the right time or get behind it, but I'm not going to stop. I'll write the next one." You can't control publishers. It's out of your hands.

Do you have any advice for aspiring writers?
TJ: If writing is what you want to do, you have to keep doing it. Sometimes even the most talented people get tired of the

constant rejection. First you get rejected by yourself. You're sitting at the typewriter thinking your writing isn't any good. Later, you get rejected by editors. It's a masochist's profession. And as I say, it's not necessarily the most talented who survive. It's the people who are the most determined to keep writing, and who are the most in love with their vocation. There are people who write a brilliant book, have it turned down because it's different or whatever, and then they give up. Someone else who's more determined might write ten terrible books. If they're willing to keep doing it, perhaps the eleventh book will be the one that's published. So the main thing is to stick with it and not give up.

Maxine Hong Kingston

Maxine Hong Kingston

Maxine Hong Kingston's remarkable book *The Woman Warrior* tells of the legends and dreams of "a girlhood among ghosts." As a young girl, Maxine Hong Kingston heard incredible stories about her Asian ancestors. In her writing, she combines these stories with fictional fantasies as well as information about Chinese history and her Chinese cultural heritage. A graduate of the University of California at Berkeley, Kingston is married and the mother of one son. Her book *China Men* won the National Book Award for nonfiction and was nominated for a National Book Critics Circle Award and a Pulitzer Prize. She is also the author of *Tripmaster Monkey—His Fake Book*.

Why do you write?
MHK: Writing orders thought. It gives meaning to life. And I create beauty and help change the atmosphere of the world.

Where does the ability to write come from?
MHK: I don't know. I think I was born with it. I've been inventing stories for as long as I can remember. It's very mysterious. It's like eating and breathing. I eat. I breathe. I write. I remember a time when I wasn't writing. I was a child and I hadn't yet learned to read. Before that, however, there was imagining and storytelling. I see writing as a very early, possibly innate impulse.

How old were you when you started to write poetry?
MHK: I was about nine when I began to write poetry. I began to record what I was thinking and speaking. I think it coincided with learning to speak English well. I spoke in Chinese, but wrote things in English.

Your language is very beautiful. Do you remember your parents' language as somewhat lyrical? Did they use poetic words when they told you the stories of your ancestors?
MHK: Their language was strong, but I don't think it was lyrical. It was powerful. They also read poetry that was beautiful. I think of their language as powerful and imaginative. They read the poems out loud and they also sang. It was part of their culture.

How did you develop your unique language?
MHK: I believe my language comes from trying to have as good an ear as possible. I try to hear the way people speak. I try for realism. If the language turns out to be beautiful, then it's beautiful. I try more for realism than for beauty. I let the beauty take care of itself. All writing has to do with translation; and I mean not only from one language to another. There are pictures, sounds, and things that happen in life, and it must be translated into words. There's a rendering that has to take place. There's room to play with the words and get them as close as possible to colors and actions. Words take on a kind of plastic quality, a moving quality. Even though I try to match the words with what I see, I realize they're just words, so I give them their own cadence and harmony.

Are you musical?
MHK: No. I don't think I'm musical at all. I read what I write aloud. I want to make sure the words sound good in the mouth and that the mouth feels good making the words. I want them to

sound correct to the ear. In that sense, words become part of the body's rhythm. Words become beautiful when they're in harmony with heartbeats and breathing and the physical way a mouth moves. It's all a part of rhythm. I guess that's what you mean by musical. Words become musical if they fit the way the physical body works. But in the sense of playing an instrument or going to concerts, I rarely understand what I'm hearing.

Could you describe your writing process?
MHK: When I'm first composing, I often write with a pencil in longhand. I write in longhand when I'm first trying to go from vision to words. Using a pencil is like sketching. It's not that committed. You can play all over the paper. I also like using my hand. I used to think I could be a painter. I enjoy sketching with a good paper and pencil. I also type. I use the typewriter when I'm trying to fill holes, and when I want to quickly see everything that's in my mind. I go very fast in order to get a whole bunch of stuff out and onto the paper. I don't always use everything, but at least I've unloaded the thoughts from my head. I also have a computer, and I use it for the later drafts. I didn't buy the computer until I was quite far along in the novel I'm writing now. I didn't know very much about computers, and I wasn't sure they were good instruments for composing.

Is writing easy for you?
MHK: No. It's not easy. I get into writing, and then the problems come within the piece. I have been doing it long enough to know that amazing solutions also come. The harder the problem, the better the solution.

Is getting through the problems part of the reason you enjoy writing?
MHK: No. I don't like that part. I like having an instrument for order and meaning in a universe that's chaotic and always

changing. It's wonderful that we have a process available for finding meaning and order, for making beauty, and for keeping track of thoughts. Writing is a medium that's just right for me. It's cheap. All you need is a paper and a pencil. It's secretive. I like that. You can be very secretive and you don't have to make any noise. The neighbors won't complain. And yet, at the same time, you are communicating with the world.

Did your books sell easily or did you have to go through rejection?
MHK: No. I didn't have any problem with that. Because I'm a good editor and critic, I didn't send my work out until it was ready. I could have sent it out often and received lots of rejections, but I knew it wasn't ready so I just waited. I think most people who receive a lot of rejections are young people who can't wait to send out their first draft as soon as it's finished. I was thirty-five years old when I sold my first novel. I also believe that reading a lot of different authors helps you become objective.

Who are your favorite authors?
MHK: I enjoy Virginia Woolf, and I like how she works with time. Lately, I've been reading biographies about women. I especially enjoy biographies about artistic women—Edith Wharton, Willa Cather, Katherine Mansfield, Georgia O'Keeffe, and Frida Kahlo. I'm interested in how these women lead their lives and how they find time to create.

Do you have any advice for young writers?
MHK: The best advice is to keep writing. Write constantly. Writing is a perfect medium for discovery. Students sometimes feel they shouldn't begin until they're inspired, but writing is a medium toward inspiration.

You write about women from your culture. What kind of a message can young women today apply to their own lives from these women from the past?

MHK: I hope that by "women from *your* culture" you mean Americans of the twentieth century—women of *our* culture. I do not want readers to think that I am writing about an exotic other world. The stories of an old country are in the background of every American. Some of my characters are trapped by history and by oppressive mores; others somehow break free. Women who were born and raised in slavery have been able to become feminists and to invent new roles and identities. They were able to do this by finding liberating myths, such as that of the woman warrior, by discovering heroines and role models, and by seeing through injustices that society takes for granted, and thus being strong enough to work hard to change the world.

THOMAS VICTOR

Norma Klein

Norma Klein

Norma Klein was well known as the author of twenty novels for young adults, as well as fourteen novels for adults. Her first book for young adults, *Mom, the Wolf Man and Me*, was published in 1972. Her first adult book, a short story collection called *Love and Other Euphemisms*, was published that same year. Included among her books are *Older Men, My Life as a Body, Lovers,* and *American Dreams*. She and her husband, who is Dean of Sciences and Mathematics at Hunter College in New York City, had two daughters: Jen, born January 3, 1967, and Katie, born June 19, 1970. Norma Klein held a B.A. from Barnard College (1960) and a Master's in Slavic Languages from Columbia (1963). This interview was conducted not long before her death in April, 1989.

Why do you write?
NK: When I was young, I received tremendous pleasure from reading. I find the idea of being able to give that particular kind of pleasure to other people very exciting. Many of the professions I considered involved escaping into an imaginary world. I feel fortunate in that society allows you to have a bad habit, daydreaming, and actually pays you for it if you can transfer those fantasies into words. Writing is a way to have many different adventures. You can become other people, change your sex, get older or younger, and you don't even have to leave your study! At the moment I'm earning a good living as a writer, but I didn't begin writing thinking of that as even a

remote possibility. I always needed some form of artistic expression. I considered becoming a painter, but that would have had all the pleasures and problems of writing: solitude, an erratic income, lack of security. I still paint and sometimes I wonder if I didn't make a mistake by not going into that field. By and large, however, I'm glad I picked writing.

As a child, were you conscious of having an imagination?
NK: Yes. I always wondered whether everyone did, and whether you had to give it up once you got married. I don't remember if I considered writing as a profession when I was a child. I think writing went hand in hand with painting, in terms of importance in my life, until I was in college. There I was influenced by the fact that Barnard offered no studio art courses but did offer creative writing. It also seemed easier to face rejection by mail, as writers do, than in person, as painters have to.

When did you actually start writing?
NK: I wrote as a child. Then, in college, I entered *Mademoiselle's* fiction contest. Even though I didn't win, they bought the story, "Helen," and published it. When I was nineteen, my first short story for adults was published in a literary magazine, *The Grecourt Review*. Until I was thirty I wrote stories for adults which appeared mainly in similar literary quarterlies: *The Sewanee Review, Prairie Schooner*. I kept trying to get a story collection published in hardcover, but editors continued to balk unless I would say I was going to write a novel. I didn't have any plans for a novel. My favorite writer is Anton Chekhov and he never wrote any novels, though he wrote six hundred short stories and many plays. I kept saying, "Never, never," and then one day I thought, "If you want to get a book of stories into print, you'd better write a novel." That was really my motivation in beginning my first novel, *Pratfalls*, in 1970.

Now I no longer write short stories and I've learned to love writing novels. What happened was that *Pratfalls*, because it was under two hundred pages, ended up in a short story collection, my first adult book, *Love and Other Euphemisms*. Around the same time, I had my first child. I was in my late twenties, and reading picture books aloud to her revived the idea of writing and illustrating my own books. I wrote a few picture book texts with accompanying illustrations and showed them to an agent. She felt that since I wasn't a professional artist, it would be difficult to get them published. Instead, she suggested I try writing a novel for eight-to-twelve-year-olds. Frankly, I never would have thought of that. But it sounded fairly simple. Novels for kids that age are usually only about one hundred pages. I thought, "What can I lose?" I wrote *Mom, the Wolf Man and Me* in two weeks in 1971, and it was published the following year. It was an instant success, the kind that has never happened to me in the adult field. As a result of that experience, I became inspired. I saw how little realistic fiction was available for young people, and I wanted to rectify that situation.

Did you read many young adult novels before you wrote one?
NK: No, I really didn't. If I had known more about the field I might not have entered it for a variety of reasons. I wasn't aware of how tremendously conservative the children's book field is. Once I became aware, I still thought it was a temporary phenomenon, that it was just a coincidence that there was so little good realistic fiction. The fact is, many writers enter the field because they're terrified of sexuality and other aspects of adult life. They try to hide in a kind of never-never land of childhood innocence. So I was immediately considered a pariah, just for dealing with topics like divorce, death, homosexuality. There are quite a few writers today who are being censored for similar reasons: Bob Cormier, Judy Blume, Harry Mazer. Problems that don't exist for adult writers are still being

ardently fought. The kind of horror the work of D.H. Lawrence evoked decades ago is still very real. Many people would simply like young people to go straight from reading *The Wind in the Willows* to Dickens. The idea that there should be an area of literature specifically for teenagers is still questioned.

The other fact that bothers me about the field is that it is and probably always will be a literary ghetto. Children's books are primarily written by women, and many of the editors in the field are women. What saddens me as a feminist is that many feminists still speak very slightingly of children's books, though they are unconsciously mimicking attitudes which are sexist in origin. Children's or young adult books are rarely reviewed at any length, they don't get much attention, and they often are excluded from major literary awards (the National Book Award stopped giving a prize for children's books some years ago). If *The New York Times Book Review* has a list of important books that are coming out in the fall or spring, it never includes young adult novels. At universities, even those with strong Women's Studies programs, few courses are offered in young adult literature, though this is a field where women have excelled from the beginning. It's a separate but extremely unequal situation.

Would you discourage young people from writing for teenagers?
NK: I told my class in "Writing Fiction with a Teenage Protagonist" at Yale in 1987 that I believe one reason people go into this field is because they want to write the books they wish they could have read as young people. I feel my books have succeeded with their audience: kids. But they mainly evoke horror in the children's book establishment and are ignored by the much more powerful adult literary community.

Anyone who wants to go into the field should realize that a reputation as a writer for young adults will be viewed as a deficit if you try to publish adult novels. I've had publishers beg me to leave my list of young adult novels off the list of my published works, when the novel is for adults. I've been told, "We had to work hard to overcome your reputation as a writer for young adults," as though this were a criminal record, following me from place to place! It's not as though you succeed in an equally respected field, nonfiction, say, and then cross over. It's more as though you had a "bad rep" in high school; you'd better be sure to go to a college far enough away so nobody knows.

I'm on the PEN [Poets, Essayists and Novelists] admissions committee, and when a writer of teenage novels applies for membership and sends in one of her books, everyone turns to me, saying, "We don't know how to judge this." When I say, in effect, "Judge it as you would an adult novel, by characterization, style, use of language," they all look puzzled. Yet a moment's glance at the book in question would have indicated no separate standards are necessary. It's also infuriating when a writer known only for adult novels publishes a book with a teenage protagonist and it's hailed with ads, blurbs, and long reviews. Similar novels by writers whose specialty this is appear all the time, but they are ignored.

How big is your audience?
NK: It's very influenced, as literature always is, by the politics of the time. When I entered this field in the early seventies, there was an overlap from the liberalism of the sixties. Now we have retreated back to the dark ages. Many current young adult novels are throwbacks to the "Will Johnny invite me to the junior prom?" type of fifties romance. In hardcover, where, like everyone else, I'm dependent on librarians, my book might sell only 5,000 to 10,000 copies. Teenagers don't buy hardcovers. But in paperback my novels can sell as many as half a million copies. Book sales are greatly affected by the politics of

publishing. If I write a young adult novel in a style adults might appreciate, it's still marketed with a cover that will ensure only being read by eleven to fourteen year-old girls. I'd like to think of myself as a writer of realistic fiction, but in fact most readers of realistic fiction will never know my books exist. Then, I've been to parts of the country where they not only want to ban my books but would gladly hang me from the nearest tree.

If some people see one four-letter word in a children's book, it shocks them, and yet the material found in adult books is no longer shocking at all. Why is this?
NK: It's a complete double standard. The irony is that sexuality is probably *the* crucial issue of the teenage years. It's more important in teenagers' lives than it will be when they're twenty or even fifty. Yet you still cannot write about sex, even about college-bound, sensitive, responsible kids having love affairs, without causing mayhem among most librarians. It's as though a black curtain has been dropped in front of a subject of vital importance. It promotes a sense of shame and ignorance. It keeps the field back, from a literary point of view.

Can you do anything about it?
NK: I hope my writing will make some small difference, but basically I don't think novels change the world. When my books are banned, I go to different parts of the country and defend them. I try and establish some type of dialogue. The problem is, most of these people haven't even read the books they're banning. They are terrified of the fact that a book can cause kids to question, to think.

Do you use humor when you're trying to make a serious point?
NK: I'm not a stand-up comic. I do have a sense of humor and it appears in my fiction, even in novels about serious subjects.

Angel Face is about a mother who commits suicide and *Going Backwards* is about a grandmother with Alzheimer's disease. A few friends remarked, "You're dealing with these grave issues, and yet there are times when I laughed out loud." I suppose it's part of the contradictory way I see the world. I consider myself a pessimist, and yet I find a lot of things in life funny.

Do young people write to you and say you've helped them?
NK: Some of my readers are growing up in communities that are quite rigid, oppressive, and anti-intellectual. I think what my books may have done for some young people is to show them there's another, more open world out there where being gay or different is not such a tragedy, and that if they can hang in there, they'll reach that world.

Is writing a good career for someone who wants children?
NK: For me it worked out extremely well. I was working, yet I was at home and accessible in terms of a major crisis. But we did spend a good part of our income on household help. I don't regret that at all. Baby-sitters allowed me to preserve my sanity, to the extent that I have. I always had at least three hours in the morning to write. I couldn't have given up writing. I think I could have enjoyed a marriage without children, though I'm very glad I had them; they've enriched my life enormously. But I don't think I could have had a satisfying life without writing. Thankfully I didn't have to make that choice.

What advice would you give young people who want to write?
NK: You must love it with a total passion. It's not enough to just want to get a book into print. That's not going to see you through a lifetime of rejection and all the other hideous frustrations writers experience. You really must believe that life would not be possible without writing.

Denise Levertov

Denise Levertov

The poet Denise Levertov was born in Essex, England. She settled in the United States and became a naturalized citizen in 1955. Her poetry addresses many subjects and often has a strong political and social theme. Her books of poetry include *The Jacob's Ladder, The Sorrow Dance, Relearning the Alphabet, To Stay Alive, Footprints, Life in the Forest, Candles in Babylon, Oblique Prayers,* and *Breathing the Water.* Her essays, criticism, and other writings are contained in such volumes as *The Poet in the World* and *Light Up the Cave.* She has taught at many colleges and universities including Vassar, M.I.T., University of California at Berkeley, University of Cincinnati, Tufts, Brandeis, and Stanford. At the age of twelve, she sent a sampling of her poetry to T.S. Eliot. He wrote back with a long letter of encouragement.

Why do you write?
DL: Because it is natural to me, the way it is natural for an oak tree to produce acorns or for a fish to swim.

When did you realize you wanted to write, and how did you develop your talent?
DL: I began to write as a very small child—about five years old, or possibly even earlier. (I had to dictate my first poems to my big sister.) What would have happened if I had not lived in a house full of books, among people who read a lot and who were

all involved in some type of writing, and if I had not been read to and heard grown-ups reading aloud to one another, it is impossible to say.

How did you choose the form your words would take? Did you ever consider becoming a novelist or playwright?
DL: The poetic form chose *me*. I did write stories as well, and still sometimes do. And of course I've written lots of nonfiction prose. I do not feel able to write novels or plays, though.

When young poets first recognize their gift, should they write with a purpose, such as to awaken social consciousness, or should they just allow the words to flow?
DL: In one sense, they should just "allow the words to flow"—but not in the sense of not ever looking at what they've written and trying to improve it by every means in their power. Their responsibility is to their gift itself, if they have one; which means that they must be willing to go beyond mere "self-expression," and make a written work that can stand free from them, a thing in itself.

What advice would you offer the young poet who is easily discouraged?
DL: If there is a strong impulse towards the art of poetry—a love of language, a love of making things of integrity out of language—the young poet will not be discouraged for long. I'd say: Don't run around showing your poems and seeking reassurance from others: live with the poems, try to see them objectively, compare the latest ones with those you wrote a year ago, and see if you've learned anything about technique while you were living through that year's changes. And above all, keep reading the great poets, past and present. Be your own teacher—but remember you will have much to learn.

Is the pleasure poets receive from sharing their art with an unseen world a reason to write?
DL: That pleasure you speak of is *not* a "reason why I write." I hope, and sincerely believe, that I would continue to write on a desert island with no expectation of rescue. The pleasure of communication, of seeing *proofs* of having communicated, is an undeniable gratification. It can be ego-stroking or humbling (maybe even both at once!). But woe betide the writer for whom it is the motivation for writing.

Do you have any additional comments?
DL: While (as I said before) it is better not to be dependent on the opinions of others, it is also important (if opportunity offers) to learn from older poets and from your peers. One of the best ways to learn from your peers is to learn to offer *them* constructive criticism. By doing this for each other, in a noncompetitive spirit, people can learn to criticize their own work constructively. A good workshop leader will share the fruits of his/her years of experience. He or she will also provide a working vocabulary for people to use when responding to each other's work. This will stop them from saying useless things like "it's nice," or "it's creepy!"

Nancy Meyers

Nancy Meyers

Nancy Meyers is a celebrated screenwriter. Her credits include *Private Benjamin* (for which she received an Academy Award nomination), *Irreconcilable Differences*, and *Baby Boom*. Her writing partner, Charles Shyer, is also her partner in life. They have two young daughters. Ms. Meyers and Mr. Shyer are involved in every aspect of their pictures. They write, he directs, and she produces each of their films.

Why do you write?
NM: That's a good question! Writing is a way for me to express myself. I write about the things I care about. The movies I write are not totally fictional. They're about issues I'm concerned with. Movies are a way for me to get things off my chest...to talk about them. Anyway, I've always been a big movie fan. Writing movies, making movies—it's a lot of fun. Charles and I try and write movies that have a classic structure. I love to watch and study old movies: classics by Ernst Lubitsch, Preston Sturges, Howard Hawks, and Billy Wilder.

What steps did you take to become a writer?
NM: I studied journalism at American University in Washington, D.C. After I left college, I went to work in public television. I soon became interested in theatrical writing, and I felt if I wanted to write, I should move to California. I got a job as a story editor. It was the best education I could have had. I

read screenplays every day and worked with writers. I spent all my time in the world of screenwriting. I actually started writing before I went to work as a story editor, but working in this job made me realize how little I really knew.

How did you get the job as story editor?
NM: I was jogging one day, and by coincidence I met a producer who was looking for a story editor. I told him I was trying to write and I wanted to learn the business. I went to work for him a few days later. After two years, the producer Ray Stark asked if I would come and do the same for him. A year later I left and wrote *Private Benjamin*.

That's a pretty amazing story. When did you meet Charles Shyer?
NM: I met him while I was a story editor. Charles was already writing films. He encouraged me to write and taught me a tremendous amount.

Why is your personality suited to working with a partner?
NM: Although I'm argumentative, I'm not competitive. I can see the value in someone else's ideas. When you collaborate, you have to put aside your ego. Anyone who's involved in a relationship knows what you have to go through to make it work. Collaboration is just another type of relationship.

Is it easier to write with a partner you live with?
NM: We have on occasion written with an outside collaborator, Harvey Miller. It was refreshing to bounce things off someone I hadn't seen since the day before. Ultimately, however, there's no one I'd rather write with than Charles.

Is it difficult separating your personal life from your work?
NM: There's nothing more personal than writing. Writing

together has strengthened our relationship. We not only share our children and our home, but also our ideas.

Is it hard to block out the pressures of success? Are you easily distracted by the social life and other benefits?
NM: We don't have a very big social life. We're not party people. To be honest, most of our friends are writers. Our friends work very hard, so we don't spend a lot of time getting together. In terms of success, I guess we're fairly insecure. We still worry we'll never work again. We always have that fear hanging over us. How will we live next year?

What was it like to receive an Oscar nomination?
NM: It was great. I don't think about it very often, however. Our first movie was so successful that at times it's easy to try and compete with that experience. Our next movie wasn't as successful, although it received better reviews and was well liked. When that happens it jumbles you immediately. I'm sure I'd be affected differently if all my movies were big hits and received nominations.

Do you work out problems in your movies or create new ones?
NM: Probably both. We write about personal things. We write about people in contemporary relationships. We wrote *Irreconcilable Differences* after *Private Benjamin*. We put some of the things we'd experienced into that movie. We wrote about how the Ryan O'Neal character related to being successful and how success changed him. We wrote about things we didn't want to happen to us. This was a way of protecting ourselves. At the time of *Private Benjamin*'s success, we did get courted a bit. Although that's not something we're attracted to, we can write about the experience.

How did you develop the business side of your personality?
NM: It wasn't hard for me because I'm basically an assertive person. Once I've written something, my main ambition is to protect it. Unlike novels, screenplays get rewritten by other writers. There's a clause in our contract that says no one can rewrite our work. If someone buys one of our scripts, they know they can't turn it over to someone else to rewrite it. We'll rewrite the script endlessly, but no one else can. In terms of selling, my agent is responsible for that side of the business. I don't think I'd be great at hustling.

Were you highly motivated as a young girl?
NM: Yes, always. I always wanted a career. I was always entranced by any movie in which the woman character had an office or a desk. I always wanted to be a professional.

Are you sensitive to criticism?
NM: I'm sensitive, but I try not to be defensive. I try to learn. Of course I react differently, depending on who's giving me the criticism. It's O.K. if a friend offers good constructive criticism. But after the project's finished and I see someone on television telling me what's wrong and solving all the problems, that kills me. I don't love it. It's hard, but my job is open to the public for criticism.

Do you watch the reviews on television?
NM: If I know we're going to be reviewed, I don't tune in. I wait to hear about it from someone else. It hurts if they say my work isn't any good. They're talking about my talent. If I hear ahead of time that the review is great, however, sure I'll tune in!

What advice would you offer someone who wants to become a screenwriter?
NM: Read screenplays. That really helped me. I read screenplays for three years. I still read the great ones. I don't think one approach to learning the business is necessarily better than another. It's also helpful to try and get something made. Start anywhere. Seeing your work produced is the best encouragement in the world.

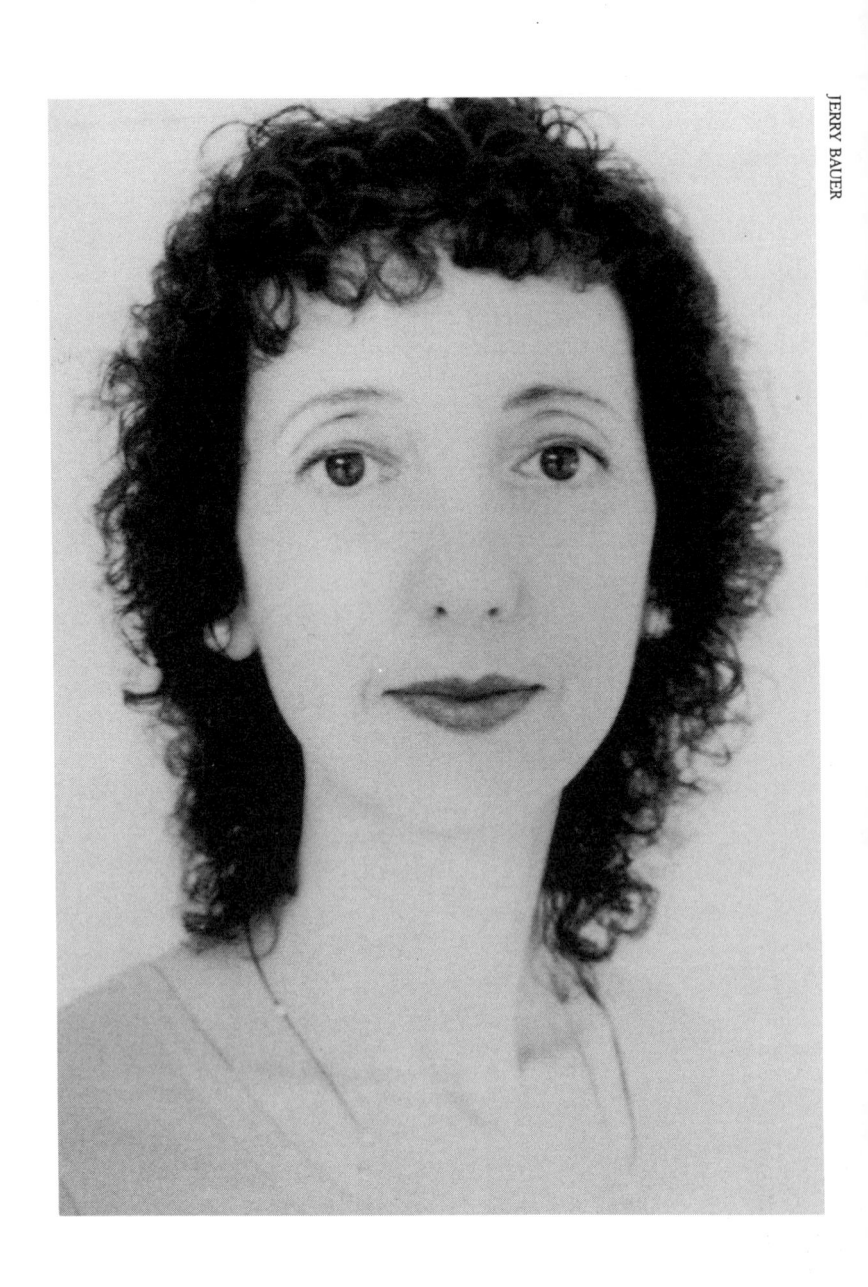

Joyce Carol Oates

Joyce Carol Oates

Joyce Carol Oates is the author of seventeen novels and many volumes of short stories, poems, and essays, as well as plays. She has been honored by awards from the Guggenheim Foundation, the National Institute of Arts and Letters, and the Lotos Club, and by a National Book Award in 1970 for her novel *them*. For many years her short stories have been included in the annual *O. Henry Prize Stories* collection, and she is the recipient of the O. Henry Special Award for Continuing Achievement. She has been a member of the American Academy and Institute of Arts and Letters since 1978. Born in Lockport, New York, Ms. Oates now lives in Princeton, New Jersey, where she is on the faculty of Princeton University. Her novels include *Do with Me What You Will, Garden of Earthly Delights, Bellefleur, You Must Remember This*, and *American Appetites*. She is also the author of a collection of essays entitled *Woman Writer: Occasions & Opportunities*.

Why do you write?
JCO: To enlarge my sympathies, and perhaps those of others; to create something (semi)-permanent; to pursue lives, experience adventures otherwise inaccessible to me. And to experiment with language, to me a continuing joy.

Please describe the physical environment in which you write. How has it changed over the years, and do you find it more difficult to block out distractions?
JCO: I write in a fairly large office/study, with much window space, and two desks—each with a typewriter: one for my writing, the other for letters and briefer projects. One wall-sized window looks out onto an atrium. Other windows look out onto a wildflower garden, and a stand of deciduous and evergreen trees. I can't say that there are more distractions now than previously, or that I have difficulty blocking them out; my writing habits, like the habits of my life, haven't changed much over the years.

Do you ever reread your early work? Does it help to look back?
JCO: Sometimes, but not for "help." I seem to work less quickly now, less fluidly, spending more time on sentences *per se*, and the choice of specific words, so when I reread early work I tend to be surprised, sometimes quite amazed, that it stands up as well as it seems to, at least in my judgment...we tend, I think, to undervalue our early efforts, believing that we can do better now. "Looking back" is a project of a kind an older, perhaps even elderly writer might begin, as a general process of reviewing an entire life.

As a young writer, did you experience rejection? If so, how did your desire to write overcome any setbacks or disappointments?
JCO: Yes, of course—to the first question. (A writer who has never experienced rejections simply has not sent his work to the right places.) The second question seems unanswerable. How...? It simply did. I have always tended to be a rather stubborn, single-minded person, like most serious writers. Also, I am willing to work very hard; *very* hard.

Have you been influenced by the work of any female authors?
JCO: A writer's influences are so varied, so incalculably heterogeneous, it's impossible to answer helpfully. I could name the Brontës, Virginia Woolf, Katherine Mansfield, Willa Cather, George Eliot, Colette...but I'm not really sure if they are influences.

How does a young writer learn to use reality as a means of provoking the imagination?
JCO: Simply look; look carefully; listen; be aware. The objective eye is precious, so that, when the subjective imagination comes into play, there is at least a bedrock of something real and unassailable beneath it.

How does advanced education benefit the writer?
JCO: No one is much interested in the thoughts or vocabularies of ill-educated people, so, naturally, an "advanced" education cannot fail to benefit the writer. (At least if he or she is hoping for a serious audience.)

What advice would you offer the young writer?
JCO: Simply do a good deal of reading in a variety of subjects; read "serious," even "difficult" books, to stretch your imagination; don't be easily discouraged, or discouraged at all. The young writer has to be aware of great, classic literature but he must also be aware of the work of his contemporaries so that he won't spend valuable time writing stories that have already been written and have passed out of fashion.

But, as I've indicated, the serious writer is stubborn, single-minded, convinced of his ability to write...hence not much in need of advice.

Carolyn See

Carolyn See

Carolyn See, who holds a Ph.D. from UCLA, has had a very diverse writing career. She is a regular book reviewer for the *Los Angeles Times.* She also contributes articles to such magazines as *Esquire, The Atlantic, Harper's, Los Angeles Magazine, Sports Illustrated,* and *T.V. Guide.* She has written four novels, including *Golden Days.* She is one-third of the popular novelist "Monica Highland"; the other two-thirds are John Espey (with whom she has lived for fourteen years) and her daughter Lisa See Kendall. They have published three books: *Lotus Land, 110 Shanghai Road,* and *Greetings from Southern California.* Carolyn See has also written, with John Espey, a collection of essays on education entitled *Two Schools of Thought.* And she has sold a television movie-of-the-week, entitled *Secrets,* to CBS.

Why do you write?
CS: When I'm doing my best work, my serious work, I really am living in a better world. I throw out all the junk, and I'm living in a better place. I might as well be pretentious and say it's very much like meditation, a form of prayer, a form of hooking up to the divine. When I'm writing just ordinary stuff, it's fun. It's like crossword puzzles or gardening.

Why did you become a writer?
CS: My father was a different kind of writer. He wrote seventy-three books of hard-core pornography before he died. He

always wanted to be a writer, and he did succeed. He wrote all these crazy books, had a really good time, and found his life's work, which was taking the fear and disgust out of sex. He didn't begin writing books until he was sixty-nine.

I always wanted to write. I remember sitting down to write my first novel in my early twenties. I didn't know what I was doing, but I remember thinking, "O.K., this is it." It was like clicking into another world. It was like going from AM to FM.

How did your career evolve?
CS: I started to write fairly seriously around the time my second marriage was breaking up. I had a three-year-old and a thirteen-year-old to support. It never occurred to me to "go to work." At that point I made the decision to earn a living as a writer. Unfortunately, my plan didn't work out very well, and after two or three years I started teaching at Loyola Marymount University in Los Angeles. Eventually I stopped teaching and began writing again. Now I'm making a good living.

In what area did you receive your Ph.D.?
CS: American literature. I wrote a huge doctoral dissertation on the Hollywood novel. It's completely unreadable, but very scholarly. It's 535 pages long.

Does advanced education help the writer, or can it be used as a way of procrastination?
CS: I can give you the completely conventional answer. There is a tradition in America that the best writers did things like chopping wood. That was their "education." In England, everyone went to Oxford or Cambridge. D.H. Lawrence was one of the only writers who came from the working class. In America, it was the other way around. If you went to college, you were a wimp. Look at Hemingway. He was a hard-boiled

reporter, Faulkner was a drunk, and Fitzgerald flunked out of Princeton. It wasn't until after World War II that our writers got a chance at an advanced education. Of course, there are some exceptions, but the vast majority of writers came from the school of hard knocks.

As soon as the GI Bill happened, people had a chance to go to school. They took advantage of the opportunity, and from 1945 on almost every writer received at least an undergraduate degree, and very often an advanced degree. Graduate school gave women the opportunity to get out of the house and into a place where they could read and not be bothered. No one could say they were wasting their time. Try and remember that America is a place where Puritan essays were written about women who read too much and went crazy. Graduate school totally validated the fact that a woman could sit down and read all day. It gave women a type of Virginia Woolf's "room," but without the money. It gave women the room to read and think and talk about books.

Many people have a dilemma—should they try and sell their writing or go to graduate school?
CS: A little of both is nice.

Is there some truth to the concept that a writer earns a living but doesn't really work?
CS: A writer is always doing piecework on some level. You're always right on the edge. There may be as few as ten writers in America that are not living on the edge.

Is the fear of a job, or a nine-to-five situation, part of the creative personality?
CS: Yes. You can see this point in the difference between writers and editors. They both love the world of letters, but

editors need a nine-to-five job. I think it has more to do with money than with just the creative process. Editors need an office. They need a place or a shelter. A lot of writers can't take that idea. A free-lance writer is someone who moves around, almost like a psychological hobo. I don't know whether that is good or bad, but I think it's definitely part of the profile of a working writer.

How did you become a book reviewer?
CS: Simply by being in town and getting a reputation for meeting deadlines. You sort of hang out with editors and writers and do your work. Someone says, "Why don't we send her a book to review?" and that's it. The most important part of reviewing books is meeting deadlines. If you take a book, wait for three months, and don't turn in a review, you won't get asked again.

Do you find it difficult to criticize other people when you yourself are a novelist?
CS: No. A critic who doesn't do his or her own work is very much like a teacher of freshman composition who doesn't write. You're always criticizing from a kind of blank plate of perfection. That is to say, your standard is "perfect" because you've never tried it yourself. It certainly takes you off your high horse if you're a working writer. If you're a regular reviewer as well as a writer, you're a lot kinder and—I think—a lot smarter than reviewers who are only reviewers.

Do you take criticism well yourself?
CS: No! I hate it, but I've learned that the best way to deal with criticism is to write everyone a thank-you note and say they've really given you some insight into your work. I write thank-you notes to everyone who gives me a bad review and to everyone

who gives me a good review. The only way to deal with it is to say thank you and move on.

Do you receive thank-you notes, too?
CS: Yes, and generally people write nice letters.

Getting reviewed is all part of being a writer, isn't that true?
CS: Yes, and though I hate to say it, a lot of the bad reviews are right. They're not just exercises in malice. The reviewer is trying to tell you what is wrong so you can become aware of the problem and fix it next time.

Do you think you can tell right away whether a student has talent?
CS: Oh no. Not at all. I'm really glad you brought that up. Talent, or whatever we call talent, is about twentieth on the list of what's important for a writer. I think courage is terribly important. In fact, it is probably the most important quality. Courage is the ability to just jump off the skyscraper and see what happens. It's a foolhardy, reckless urge to tell the truth no matter what happens.

Do you therefore believe people can develop the qualities that will make them succeed at writing?
CS: Of course. I also believe if you hook up that courage, give yourself a focus, and add ambition, you're in business.

What is a writer's greatest handicap?
CS: Fear. Some people feel a lack of self-esteem in their lives. If you're lucky, it won't carry over to your writing.

What is the best way to dive in?
CS: Just do it. What I say in my classes and what I try to practice in my own life is: Write a thousand words a day, make

one charming phone call, and write one charming note. There are a lot of people who sit around wringing their hands and saying, "Oh, I just couldn't do that." I think that's a lot of garbage. I must say, however, these rules are easy to make but hard to follow.

Do you think writer's block and other problems for writers are somewhat conditioned?
CS: Many people think a writer is supposed to suffer, wear elbow patches, have a tweed jacket and all the other "writer" stuff. But you can really have it any way you want. Instead of saying you have writer's block, you can just as easily say, "My ideas come faster than I can write them down."

Do you think it's important for a writer to "network"?
CS: That's why I advise the "one charming note" and "one charming phone call." When I started writing, I was terribly shy, but I had to get over it. The ability to find a market for your work is as important as your talent. Do you know where your piece is going? Do you know where you want to be in five years and how you're going to get to that point? A lot of people don't want to "know" this material, but I just came back from doing a five-day stint at a small liberal arts college in the middle of the country where a lot of grown men and women were absolutely convinced that "merit" and merit alone accounts for a writer's success. They were appalled by the idea that people like Raymond Carver or even John Irving might go out on the road to promote their books. That of course justifies them in taking a position of complete passivity with regard to their own literary careers. I suppose the next thing to say would be, That's why they've got a lot of unpublished novels turning yellow in the closet, stuck somewhere under their golf shoes.

What advice do you offer young writers?
CS: Write what you're crazy about. The only thing not to do is write what you think someone else wants you to write. You'll never win that game. You'll always be mad because even if you succeed in pleasing someone else, you won't have pleased yourself. If you write what you really love and you keep sending it out, you'll be fine. Nothing bad can happen. Even if you get rejected, you will have written about something that's important to you. If you've done your best, you're home free. Your side is taken care of. You're already a success.

Anne Tyler

Anne Tyler

Anne Tyler was born in Minneapolis, Minnesota, and grew up in Raleigh, North Carolina. She graduated from Duke University at the age of nineteen. A member of Phi Beta Kappa, she pursued graduate work in Russian studies at Columbia University. Tyler is the author of eleven novels, including *Celestial Navigation, Searching for Caleb, Dinner at the Homesick Restaurant, The Accidental Tourist,* and *Breathing Lessons* (winner of the 1989 Pulitzer Prize). Her stories have appeared in such magazines as the *New Yorker,* the *Saturday Evening Post, Redbook, McCall's,* and *Harper's.* Tyler is married to a psychiatrist, Taghi Modarressi, and she and her husband live in Baltimore, Maryland, with their two daughters.

Why do you write?
AT: I like the feeling writing gives me of entering other people's lives—lives I'd never otherwise have had the chance to live.

When did you realize you wanted to write, and how did you develop your talent?
AT: I don't think I ever consciously decided to be a writer; I more or less backed into it. When I was a small child I used to whisper stories to myself in bed at night in which I'd pretend to be various other people—a woman named Dolores with eighteen children, I remember, and a girl going west in a covered

wagon—and I think of writing as a continuation of that storytelling.

What mistakes did you make, if any?
AT: In my early books, the first four, I made the mistake of thinking that to rewrite showed a lack of spontaneity. Those books are just first drafts, therefore; and looking back on them I can see now that they are loosely and sloppily written, and that I never truly sank into those lives the way I did in later books where I revised more.

How do you write? Please describe your creative process.
AT: I begin in a very mechanical and uninspired way, simply deciding that it's time I got down to another book. I think about what kind of characters would appeal to me—maybe someone I've glimpsed on a street corner and wondered about, some little human interest item in a newspaper—and then I ponder those characters a while. After that, I go through my box of index cards on which I've jotted things down over the years—a scrap of overheard conversation, a dream, a "what if?" sort of daydream, a line from a song. Some of these cards are inert (I'll think, yes, that's interesting, but it doesn't interest me *now*) and I'll put them back in the box. Others sort of flower in my mind; I'll think, Oh! I'd forgotten that, and wouldn't it be something if the answer to that scrap of conversation, for instance, were to be such-and-such. Those cards I put aside. They amount to maybe a two-inch stack. I'll sift through them awhile, trying to find a connection between all those disparate elements, and that connection is my plot.

How do you begin your novels?
AT: Before actually starting on the novel, I write a paragraph telling myself what it's about, in the most general way. Then I

write a page-long study of each major character, including things about him that might never appear in the novel but that could influence how he behaves, and after that a brief outline—just a phrase or sentence for each chapter saying what I think will be happening at that point. This outline can change, of course, as I go along and as my characters take over; but at least I can *imagine* I know how the book will proceed. The whole prewriting process takes about a month.

What time of day do you write?
AT: I work best in the mornings. I write in very small print on unruled white paper with a Parker Accountant Fine Point fountain pen and black ink. That seems important to me—I suspect that if I got arthritis in my right hand or, Lord forbid, lost my pen (whose point is not manufactured anymore) I would have to look for other employment. The finished product I type up on a word processor at the end of every day or so, but I rely on longhand for revision. Each novel is written out completely in longhand at least three times, not counting the page-by-page rewriting that occurs as I go along.

Do you show your work to anyone before it's finished?
AT: I don't show anyone the book before it is finished, and I don't talk about it. I love being in the middle of a book but hate finishing it, and find myself so dreading the moment when someone else will have to read it that I temporize with all kinds of silly excuses as I near the end.

How did your childhood or any other experiences influence your work?
AT: I think the fact that I had a fairly isolated childhood influenced me considerably. I was raised in a sort of commune arrangement, without many other children; I learned to be

alone and to entertain myself by imagining, and when I left the commune (at the age of eleven) I looked at the regular world from an unusually distant vantage point.

Does writing come easily to you? How do you get past the blocks or uninspired times?
AT: The *start* of writing—both starting a new book as a whole and starting in to work each morning—comes very hard. And it's seldom downright easy, but I have learned over the years to be calm and patient, and to accept that if it doesn't come today, it will come tomorrow. When I hit a real block, I find it's usually because I've taken a wrong turn—said something false or made a character do what he doesn't want to do. My remedy for that (if I can't see right off where the wrong turn occurred) is to back up a page or two and begin copying that section in longhand all over again. Usually my fingers will locate the bad spot even if my eyes didn't.

How does the pressure of success and recognition affect the writer? Does this hinder or help the creative process?
AT: I don't think *any* consciousness of public reaction, whether it's positive or negative, is good for writers. For this reason I don't read my reviews and I don't give interviews or speeches or go to public literary events—all occasions that would remind me that someone out there is judging these private daydreams that I'm writing down.

Do you think women's fiction is characteristically "female" in any way?
AT: I suppose there is a certain kind of book—more interior, more detailed, less action-oriented—that is more likely to have been written by women; but I can think of any number of such books that happen to have been written by men instead.

What advice would you give young writers? How should they develop their talent?
AT: Read, read, read. And revise, revise, revise. And don't hurry to show your work for advice and comment; your best critic is yourself, a day or a month later.

5

You, the Writer

When you decide to become a writer, you enter a maze with your eyes wide open. Each story, novel, poem, or play is a puzzle, and only you can write your way out of it. Whether you write strictly for pleasure or for both pleasure and profit, you open yourself to unlimited possibilities. Writing affords a curious individual the perfect opportunity to learn. You can research a specific project, interview interesting people, travel on assignment, or work out an idea in your own mind. There are endless opportunities to add to your mind's library of knowledge.

Writing is not a profession you can leave behind at the office. Even if you write for your own amusement, you're always on the lookout for new inspiration. Many writers carry a notebook to jot down ideas. It's not uncommon for writers to sleep with a notepad by their bedside. Many great ideas have come in the middle of a dream or during the wide awake frustration of insomnia.

This chapter will explore some realities of a writer's life. You can begin by asking yourself: Why do you write?

Must You Write?

When a young poet asked the great writer Rainer Maria Rilke what qualifications were necessary to call oneself a writer, Rilke replied, "Ask youself in the stillest hour of your night: *Must* I write? Delve into yourself for a deep answer. And if this should be affirmative, if you may meet this earnest question with a strong and simple 'I *must,*' then build your life according to this necessity."

Although your reasons for becoming a writer may not be as profound as Rilke suggests, you should nevertheless have some idea why you are drawn to this profession.

Writing is hard work. You put in many hours and you sacrifice the opportunity of pursuing a more dependable and profitable occupation. A writing career makes many demands. If outside reinforcement is what you're after, you should know that it may take many years to become established. It's an unfortunate fact that most writers earn between five and ten thousand dollars a year from their writing.

So why do you want to write? What do you hope to gain from your craft?

The ability to write is a gift that should be nurtured. It's enormously gratifying to develop an original idea, bring life to characters, or write about politics, science, or psychology. The possibilities of language are infinite, and writing gives you the opportunity to unravel and use this fascinating word game. Once you declare yourself a writer, part of your soul is committed forever.

Developing Your Gift

The only way to sharpen your writing skills is to write. Keeping a journal will allow you to write honestly and without fear of criticism. Privacy is one of the advantages of writing in a journal. You don't have to keep an exact log of your every activity. You can record thoughts, impressions of experiences, and emotions.

A journal offers a useful method of expanding and exercising your creative potential. It's not necessary to write in a small, pre-organized journal. The experience will seem more personal if you use an unlined notebook and practice sketching spontaneous ideas. You can compose poetry or just write a few short sentences. This free-form technique will help you discover your unique style of writing. A journal will also enable you to understand your emotions and allow you to reflect on your day-to-day adventures. Throughout history, many writers have kept diaries and journals.

Many early writers became aware of their interest in words through correspondence. In fact, some of the earliest novels were written in the form of letters. Even though this is an age of instant communication, the letter is still a valuable method of sharing one's thoughts. Since it may seem strange to write letters to friends you see every day, you can correspond with an out-of-town relative or become acquainted with someone from another country by joining an international pen-friend organization. You can learn a great deal about another culture by exchanging ideas with someone in Europe, Asia, Australia, or South America.

Whether you visit a pen-friend on the other side of the world or take a trip to a neighboring city, record your experiences in a travel diary. If you take a summer vacation or weekend trip, keep a separate journal for the purpose of writing about people and places you encounter during your travels. Don't just write a boring "Got up, ate lunch, saw the Grand Canyon" type of travelogue. Expand your impressions of sites and situations that are unique to your adventure. When you read your journal in a few years, you'll have vivid memories to look back on.

You should also keep a notebook containing possible story

ideas and other information you can refer to in the course of your work. If you meet people whose qualities are worth remembering for some future story, briefly describe their appearance in your notebook. You can also collect names for future characters. If you read or hear an unusual name, write it down. Make combinations of first, middle, and last names you'd like to use in your novel or short story. Titles for future projects are also worth collecting.

You should begin to save interesting stories that appear in the newspaper or in magazines. You might be able to incorporate the information into your own story or nonfiction piece. It can also be useful to collect well-written essays and articles. Keep your eyes open for information you might someday employ in your writing.

If you decide to submit your writing for outside criticism, you might consider entering one of the many contests open to young writers. The winners of these contests often receive cash prizes as well as the opportunity to be published in a national magazine. Ask your librarian for a list of current contests. Many popular magazines have annual fiction contests. There are also local and national organizations that sponsor essay-writing contests.

Most writers express mixed feelings about the value of writing classes. On the positive side, a writing class will force you to write and will provide some objective criticism. The main disadvantage is that if you haven't written before and you lack confidence in your style, you might be overly influenced by the opinion of your teacher. A writer without confidence can be extra sensitive to criticism. Classes can also be valueless if you write merely to please a teacher and select topics that don't really interest you.

Many high schools have writing classes and writing clubs. There are also community-sponsored poetry workshops as well as junior colleges and universities that offer extension classes in many areas of writing.

Writing for the school newspaper can be a very valuable experience. Many high schools and colleges also have literary magazines. If you plan to study journalism or creative writing in college, ask your counselor to direct you to the school catalogs that list specific requirements. If you plan to become a screenwriter, investigate one of the several universities that have excellent film departments.

Classes in a specific type of writing, such as screenwriting, can be very beneficial. These programs train you to write in the language of television and film. Writing that involves a definite format such as broadcast journalism, screenwriting, advertising, or newspaper reporting demands a certain expertise in the professionally accepted writing styles.

Only you can determine whether you wish to take a class in writing or work on your own. If you take a class, remember: Whether your teacher dismisses your writing as worthless or gives you an A-plus for originality, no one person is an absolute judge of a creative art. You must also be your own teacher and make honest judgments about your work. If you decide to take your writing out of the classroom and into the world of publishing, your work will produce many different responses during your career and perhaps for centuries to come!

One of the best ways to study writing is to read the work of other writers. Don't limit yourself only to your favorite authors. You should broaden your knowledge to include history, psychology, and other nonfiction. You should also read the great classic novels (including foreign authors in their native language or in translations) as well as popular fiction. Make a point of keeping up-to-date on current events. It's important to read a wide range of magazines that include news, general interest, short fiction, and essays. There are also many small literary publications that feature short stories and essays. In addition, you may want to become familiar with periodicals such as *Publisher's Weekly* and *Writer's Digest.*

One of the best ways to gain insight into the craft of writing is by reading autobiographies and biographies of writers. You can learn about their different writing processes, and you can identify with the successes and failures all writers experience during their careers. Additionally, becoming familiar with a writer's life will help illuminate that author's fiction or nonfiction.

The *Paris Review* series offers a wonderful collection of interviews with writers. The magazine dates back to the 1950s, and selected interviews are bound together in the library. Current issues are also available.

Many bookstores have book-signing parties. You can talk with popular authors, and they will autograph their books. Sometimes an author will also give a brief lecture and then respond to questions. Writers frequently speak on college campuses, and in many towns writers participate in community-sponsored lecture series. You can learn a great deal about any profession by talking with people who have already chosen this field as their vocation. Ask questions. You can save a lot of time and possible aggravation by asking people who have learned through experience.

Every writer and aspiring writer should become well acquainted with the local library. Learn how to use reference material and learn how to ask questions of your librarian. The library is free, and it contains a wealth of information that's indispensable to a writer.

The Writing Process

Discipline is a writer's best friend, and the lack of it can become a writer's worst enemy. Having great ideas means nothing if you're not disciplined enough to get them out of your mind and onto paper.

What is discipline? It's having the ability to focus on a task and stick with it. It's not easy to block out distractions and force yourself to concentrate. Discipline means clearing your mind of thoughts that can sneak into your subconscious and derail your train of thought.

Writers rarely have time clocks to punch or task-masters standing over their shoulder saying, "Get to work!" Most writers do their writing at home. They make their own hours, and the only time they have to answer to anyone is when they're working under a deadline. When you work for yourself, it's easy to find hundreds of distractions without ever leaving the house. You can waste an entire day making phone calls, running errands, and getting your photo album in order. Writers must learn to push everything out of their minds and concentrate on an $8\frac{1}{2}" \times 11"$ piece of paper.

A writer must set aside specific hours for working. Without a routine, you end up squeezing five or ten unproductive minutes into every two or three hours. And you end up with nothing but frustration.

Once you realize that discipline is the key to success and the end of stress, you'll take the time to set up a work schedule. Many writers get up very early and write before the phone starts to ring and before they become involved in other distracting tasks. If you go to school or have another job, you might be able to grab one or two hours in the early morning. If you'd prefer to sleep late, you can work after dinner when you're relatively free from interruptions. The evening is often a good time to edit the pages you've written in the morning. The hours in between give you a chance to develop a little objectivity.

While there is no set formula for developing a writing schedule, it's your responsibility to plan a routine that will work for you. Start with a quiet place where it's easy to concentrate. Some people write at a desk, while others compose in a comfortable chair. Some writers use a typewriter or a word processor, while others write everything in longhand and then type the pages into a more finished draft. Some writers dictate into a tape recorder and then pay a typist to transcribe their thoughts onto paper. Ernest Hemingway stood at a podium and wrote as if he were giving a speech or painting at an easel.

When you're developing ideas for a novel or screenplay, some teachers recommend writing your thoughts on 3" × 5" cards. Retrieving the information from cards is often easier than looking through hundreds of tiny bits of paper scattered all over the house. Looking for your notes in cluttered drawers and in messy stacks of paper can cause you to waste time and lose your creative energy.

Notebooks too can help you get organized. No matter how messy you are by nature, the pages of the notebook will somehow remain together. There's a story about a well-known writer who carried the rough draft of a novel in the trunk of her car for several years. At least she knew where to find the notes and unfinished chapters when she was ready to resume work. You can stash notes in the back of a desk or even on the shelf in a closet. One day you might run across an outline and say, "That was a good idea. Why didn't I finish it?" It's also helpful to keep a file of new ideas. You can keep your folders in a metal file cabinet or a cardboard box. Each time you come up with a new idea, label a folder and simply slip any small bits of paper inside the file. This method allows you to write on the backs of envelopes, phone messages, or whatever, and still be organized. If you're the type of person who likes to see everything in plain sight, get a bulletin board and tack your notes to it for easy viewing.

There are no rules for becoming a writer. The fields of law, medicine, and engineering teach specific procedures for becoming more effective. But a creative art can't be taught. You can only try to develop methods that help you extract more from the creative process. Creativity plus discipline is the only equation that adds up to productivity. "To be is to do" is a saying that should hang on every writer's wall. The only way to become a better writer and develop an efficient writing process is to try it out and make it work for you.

What Will You Write?

If you plan on becoming a writer, you may have already decided upon the form your words will take. You may select one type of creative writing and pursue it throughout your life, or you may discover your specialty as you explore the possibilities of each very different style of writing.

There are two major categories of writing: fiction and nonfiction. You can create a world in your imagination or you can write about the "real" world. Fiction includes such diverse genres as novels, short stories, poetry, plays, screenplays, song lyrics, teleplays, and children's stories. Nonfiction includes such equally diverse possibilities as magazine articles, advertising copy, newspaper pieces, nonfiction books, editorial essays, biographies, and television and film documentaries.

How do you decide which area to pursue? Many writers believe the "form chooses the writer" and not vice versa. Different personalities seem better suited to different forms of writing. Each type of writing requires a unique discipline and each genre presents its own spectrum of demands. If you are a private person and enjoy your own company for days on end, your temperament might be best suited to writing poetry or novels. If you need more interaction with people, you might consider becoming a newspaper reporter or a nonfiction writer for magazines, books, or screenplays. Nonfiction writers must often conduct interviews and do research that takes them away from their desks.

"Free-lance" is a term that aptly describes many writers who may write about anything and everything in an attempt to earn a living doing the thing they love most: writing. Many free-lance writers work on more than one project at a time. It's not uncommon for a free-lance writer to be working on a magazine article or newspaper piece while at the same time preparing a screenplay or novel. A free-lance writer is like a handyman, available to do any job with the same basic tools of writing. The diversity represented by a free-lance writer's resume might catch the eye of any number of possible employers.

If you wish to pursue a specific area of writing, do a little investigative reporting and ask questions. If you want to work on a newspaper, visit your local paper and talk to several reporters. Find out how they got started and ask them what they believe are the pros and cons of their field.

You can write to most authors in care of their publishers. If you want to become a novelist, ask questions and gain some first-hand insight into writing fiction.

Magazine writing can be a lucrative and exciting career for a writer. By working for a magazine, you're plunged into such diverse areas as fashion, architecture, sports, news, cooking, politics, science, and psychology. You're involved in the field, and you're able to write at the same time. A magazine offers a fast-paced, highly competitive, and pressured environment. It also enables young writers to make contacts, travel, and most importantly meet deadlines and perfect their writing skills.

Many writers with a knack for poetry enter the field of advertising. Writing copy for television or print is similar to composing limericks. Using only a few words, you must make each thought very concise and capable of carrying an important message.

If you seriously wish to become a writer, you will probably not be deterred by any negative comments you hear. Each person follows a different path to achieve his or her own goals. There is no set course. If you know which area you wish to pursue, there's no better time than now to get started. You can always move on to another genre, but if your heart leads you toward writing poetry, a novel, a screenplay, or any other form of literature, you won't ever feel truly content until you make up your mind and go for it!

The Write Traits

There's a lot more to writing than putting thoughts on paper. In addition to cultivating word skills, you should be aware of certain personality traits that will help you gain competence and achieve your goals as a writer.

Drive

There's a great deal of truth to the saying "Success is two parts drive and one part talent." It's no secret that many talented people lack the determination to turn their dreams into reality. If you wish to become a writer, you must throw away your preconceptions. You have no idea what, if any, obstacles you will encounter. Creative fields are very personal. As you have discovered in the previous biographies and interviews, each individual's story of success or failure is totally unique. The only guarantee you have is that without drive, you will not attain your goals. Achieving your goals as a writer does not necessarily mean becoming a financial success. It takes an enormous amount of drive just to see a project through from beginning to end. And it takes another surge of determination to enter the professional arena. No amount of luck can compensate for a lack of drive.

Confidence

If you lack confidence in yourself and in your work, you will probably not survive as a writer. You must have sufficient faith in your ideas to pursue a project from start to finish. When you're first developing an idea, you must have enough confidence to keep going. You cannot be discouraged every time you approach a difficult chapter or scene. And once you finish your project, you'll need confidence to show your work to other people. Most importantly, if your work is criticized or rejected, you'll need confidence to go back to the drawing board and revise or begin a new project.

Objectivity

Confidence and objectivity work together to balance your perspective as a writer. You must be able to stand back from your work and be honest about its good and bad points. You must also be able to listen to the advice of people you trust and to decide which suggested changes you should accept and which you should disregard.

The more you write, the more objective you will become. Your grammar will improve and you'll become familiar with your own unique style. You'll become your own editor and critic.

It's important to look at your work as though it had been written by someone else. You must be able to give yourself an honest compliment and also to know when a portion should be rewritten or thrown out altogether.

Patience and Persistence

Patience is right at the top of the list of qualities every writer should strive for. When you begin a project, "the end" could be six hundred pages down the road. You'll need a lot of patience to stick with the sometimes grueling task of chiseling out a sentence on the page in front of you.

If you become a professional writer, you will sometimes have to wait many months between submitting a project and receiving an answer. Then you must wait several additional months before you see your work in print.

A serious writer is not a person who gives up easily. It's important to be persistent with your craft and with the people with whom it brings you in contact. When researching facts or pursuing interviews, it's often necessary to keep looking and continue calling until you find your fact or contact your source. If your book or poem needs rewriting, you must work on it until it's right—even if that requires another two hundred or more hours of your life.

Writing involves a personal commitment. As you develop your skills, you'll begin to set standards for your work. Patience and persistence will enable you to meet your goals and push yourself toward new ideals.

Love of Language

Writing is a game of words. By perfecting your writing skills, you enhance your ability to extract meaning and express ideas through grammar, syntax, punctuation, and sentence structure.

Writing and painting are two very similar crafts. Rather than choosing colors and shapes to express a concept, a writer picks adjectives, nouns, and verbs to paint a unique picture. Just as a painter interprets an image on canvas, a writer portrays life with a unique vision or point of view.

The women writers of the past understood the power of language. The contemporary writers interviewed on these pages continue to use fiction and nonfiction to express a wide variety of opinions and ideas. The words of these writers are part of your heritage. The essays, articles, novels, poems, screenplays, and plays that will influence a new generation belong to you, the writer of tomorrow. The future is in your words.

Suggested Further Reading

Bell, Quentin. *Virginia Woolf: A Biography.* New York: Harcourt Brace Jovanovich, 1972.

Christie, Agatha. *An Autobiography.* New York: Dodd, Mead, 1977.

Frank, Anne. *The Diary of a Young Girl.* New York: Doubleday & Co., 1967.

Gilbert, Sandra M., and Gubar, Susan. *The Norton Anthology of Literature by Women: The Tradition in English.* New York: W. W. Norton & Co., 1985.

Hansberry, Lorraine. *To Be Young, Gifted and Black.* Adapted by Robert Nemiroff. Englewood Cliffs, New Jersey: Prentice-Hall, 1969.

Honan, Park. *Jane Austen: Her Life.* New York: St. Martin's Press, 1987.

Hufstader, Alice Anderson. *Sisters of the Quill.* New York: Dodd, Mead, 1978.

Laski, Marghanita. *George Eliot.* New York: Thames and Hudson Literary Lives, 1973.

May, Rollo. *The Courage to Create.* New York: W. W. Norton & Co., 1975.

Moers, Ellen. *Literary Women: The Great Writers.* New York: Oxford University Press, 1977.

Plimpton, George, editor. *Writers at Work: Paris Review Series.* 7 vols. New York: Viking Press, 1957-1986.

Rilke, Rainer Maria. *Letters to a Young Poet.* Translation by M. D. Herter Norton. New York: W. W. Norton & Co., 1934.

Wolff, Cynthia Griffin. *Emily Dickinson.* New York: Alfred A. Knopf, 1987.

For Additional Reading at Your Library:

Dictionary of Literary Biography. A Bruccoli Clark Book. Gale Research Company, Detroit, Michigan.

Contemporary Authors Autobiography Series. Gale Research Company, Detroit, Michigan.

Index

Academy Awards, 91, 123
Accidental Tourist, The, 139
Adam Bede, 24, 28
Advertising copywriting, 150, 156
Am I Blue, 91
American Academy and Institute of Arts and Letters, 122
American Appetites, 127
American Dad, 97, 98
American Dreams, 109
Angel Face, 115
Austen, Cassandra, 18–19, 20, 21
Austen, Edward, 20
Austen, George, 18, 19–20
Austen, Henry, 21
Austen, Jane, 15, 17–21, 28

Baby Boom, 121
Behn, Aphra, 9, 11
Bell, Clive, 39
Bell, Currer and Ellis. *See* Brontë, Charlotte and Emily
Bellefleur, 127
Beresford, Bruce, 93
Between the Acts, 43
Black Feeling, Black Talk, 75
Black issues, 57–60, 79–80
Black Judgment, 75

Blackwood, John, 27–28
Bloomsbury, 38, 39
Book reviewing, 131, 134
Brabant, Dr. Robert Henry, 25–26
Bray, Charles, 25
Breathing Lessons, 139
Breathing the Water, 117
Broadway, 57, 58, 59
Brontë, Charlotte, 12, 23, 28
Brontë, Emily, 12, 23, 28
Browning, Elizabeth Barrett, 12, 43
Buck, Pearl, 12
Burney, Fanny, 9
Byrne, David, 91

Candles in Babylon, 117
Cannibal in Manhattan, A, 97, 100
Caught in the Crossfire, 83
Celestial Navigation, 139
Censorship, 111–112, 114
Chapman, John, 26
Chekhov, Anton, 110
China Men, 103
Christie, Agatha, 15, 51–55
Christie, Archibald, 52–53, 54
Christie, Rosalind, 53
Collaboration, 121–122
Concentration camps, 48–49

Cotton Candy on a Rainy Day, 75
Crimes of the Heart, 91
Cross, John Walter, 29
Crown Publishers, 98, 100

D'Albert-Durade, François, 26
Daniel Deronda, 29
de Beauvoir, Simone, 60
Debutante Ball, The, 91
Deledda, Grazia, 12
Detective stories, 51–55
Diaries and journals, 11, 14, 59, 65, 93, 147–148
Diary of a Young Girl, The, 45, 46, 47–48
Dickens, Charles, 28, 29
Dickinson, Austin, 32
Dickinson, Edward, 32
Dickinson, Emily, 15, 31–35
Dickinson, Emily Norcross, 32
Dickinson, Lavinia, 31, 32
Dinesen, Isak, 12
Dinner at the Homesick Restaurant, 139
Do with Me What You Will, 127
Drinking Gourd, The, 59
Du Bois, W.E.B., 57, 59
Duckworth, George, 39
Duckworth, Gerald, 39
Duckworth, Stella, 39
Dussel, Albert, 47, 49

Egerton, Thomas, 20–21
Ego Tripping and Other Poems for Young Readers, 75
Eighteenth-century literature, 9–10
"Elinor and Marianne." See *Sense and Sensibility*
Eliot, George, 15, 23–29
Eliot, T.S., 42, 117
Emerson, Ralph Waldo, 25
Emma, 21
Epistolary. See Letter-writing
Espey, John, 131
Evans, Christiana, 24
Evans, Christiana Pearson, 24, 25
Evans, Isaac, 24, 27
Evans, Mary Ann. See Eliot, George
Evans, Robert, 24, 25, 26
Evelina, 9

Felix Holt, the Radical, 29
Feminism, 8, 10, 42–43, 60, 107, 112

Fiction, 154
   See also specific titles
"First Impressions." See *Pride and Prejudice*
Flush, 43
Footprints, 117
Forster, E.M., 42
Frank, Anne, 15, 45–49
Freedom, 57
Freud, Sigmund, 42

Garcia, Dawn, 65–73
Garden of Earthly Delights, 127
Gemini; an Extended Autobiographical Statement, 75
Gestapo. See Nazis
Giovanni, Nikki, 75–81
Going Backwards, 115
Golden Days, 131
Goodwin, Jan, 83–89
Grant, Duncan, 40
Grecourt Review, The, 110
Greetings from Southern California, 131
Guggenheim Awards, 91, 127

Hansberry, Lorraine, 15, 57–60
Hansberry, William Leo, 59
Harper's, 131, 139
"Helen," 110
Henley, Beth, 91–95
Higginson, Thomas Wentworth, 35
Highland, Monica. See Carolyn
Hogarth Press, The, 41–42
"Hours, The," See *Mrs. Dalloway*
Hughes, Langston, 57
Hurston, Zora Neale, 12

"In Defense of the Equality of Men," 60
Irreconcilable Differences, 121, 123

Jacob's Ladder, The, 117
Jacob's Room, 41
James, Henry, 29
Janowitz, Tama, 97–101
Journalism, 65–73, 83–89, 150, 155–156

Kendall, Lisa See, 131
Keynes, John Maynard, 40
Kingston, Maxine Hong, 103–107
Klein, Norma, 109–115

Ladies' Home Journal, 83
Lagerlöf, Selma, 11–12
Lane, John, 53
Les Blancs, 59
Letter-writing, 9, 14, 19, 32, 34–35, 148
Levertov, Denise, 117-119
Lewes, George Henry, 26–29
Lewis, Maria, 25
Life in the Forest, 117
Light Up the Cave, 117
Lord, Otis P., 34
Lotos Club, 127
Lotus Land, 131
Love and Other Euphemisms, 109, 111
Lovers, 109
Lucky Spot, The, 91

Mademoiselle, 110
Magazine writing, 155–156
Mallowan, Max, 55
Manhattan Theatre Club, 92
Mansfield, Katherine, 42
Mansfield Park, 21
McCall's, 139
Meyers, Nancy, 121–125
Middlemarch, 24, 29
Mill on the Floss, The, 28
Miller, Agatha Mary Clarissa. *See* Christie, Agatha
Miller, Clara, 51–52
Miller, Frederick, 51
Miller, Harvey, 122
Miller, Madge, 52, 53
Miss Firecracker Contest, The, 91
Mistral, Gabriela, 12
Modarressi, Taghi, 139
Modesto Bee, 66
Mom, the Wolf Man and Me, 109, 111
Mousetrap, The, 51
Mrs. Dalloway, 41
Murray, John, 21
My Life as a Body, 109
Mysterious Affair at Styles, The, 53
Mystery stories, 51–55

National Book Award, 103, 112, 127
National Book Critics Circle Award, 103
National Endowment for the Arts, 97
National Institute of Arts and Letters, 127
Nazis, 43, 45, 46, 47, 49
Nemiroff, Robert, 59

New York Drama Critics Circle Award, 57, 91
New York Times Book Review, The, 112
New Yorker, 98, 100, 139
Nicolson, Harold, 42
Night and Day, 41
Nin, Anaïs, 1, 12
Nineteenth-century literature, 10–11
Nobel Prize in Literature, 11–12
Nobody's Fool, 91
Nom de plume. See Pseudonyms
Northanger Abbey, 19–20, 21

Oates, Joyce Carol, 127–129
Oblique Prayers, 117
O'Casey, Sean, 57–58
O. Henry Prize Stories, 137
O. Henry Special Award for Continuing Achievement, 127
Older Men, 109
110 Shanghai Road, 131
O'Neal, Ryan, 123
Oregon Journal, 66
Orlando, 42

PEN (Poets, Essayists and Novelists), 113
Persuasion, 21
Pioneer life, 11
Playwriting, 57–59, 91–95
Poet in the World, The 117
Poetry, 31–35, 75–81, 117–119, 155
Poirot, Hercule, 53
Prairie Schooner, 110
Pratfalls, 110–111
Pride and Prejudice, 17, 19, 21
Princeton University, 97
Private Benjamin, 121, 122, 123
Pseudonyms, 8, 23, 55
Pulitzer Prizes, 91, 92, 95, 103, 139

Queen Victoria, 29

Raisin, 58
Raisin in the Sun, A, 57, 58
Redbook, 139
Relearning the Alphabet, 117
Rilke, Rainer Maria, 146–147
Robeson, Paul, 57
Romola, 28–29
Room of One's Own, A, 8, 42, 43

Index

Sachs, Nelly, 12
Sackville-West, Vita, 42
"Sad Fortunes of the Reverend Amos Barton, The," 27–28
San Francisco Chronicle, 65, 66
Sand, George, 12, 28
Saturday Evening Post, 139
Scott, Sir Walter, 24
Screenwriting, 92–93, 99, 121–125, 131–135
Searching for Caleb, 139
Second Sex, The, 60
Secrets, 131
See, Carolyn, 131–137
Sense and Sensibility, 18, 19, 20–21
Seventeenth-century literature, 9
Sewanee Review, The, 110
Shyer, Charles, 121, 122–123
Sign in Sidney Brustein's Window, The, 58
Silas Marner, 28
Sixteenth-century literature, 8
Slaves of New York, 97, 98
Sorrow Dance, The, 117
Spencer, Herbert, 26
Stark, Ray, 122
Stein, Gertrude, 12
Stephen, Adrian, 38, 39–40
Stephen, Julia Duckworth, 38, 39
Stephen, Sir Leslie, 38–39
Stephen, Thoby, 38, 39
Stephen, Venessa, 38, 39, 43
Stephen, Virginia. *See* Woolf, Virginia
Stowe, Harriet Beecher, 10, 28
"Susan." *See Northanger Abbey*

Thackeray, William Makepeace, 27–28, 29, 38
Theater. *See* Playwriting
them, 127
Those Who Ride the Night Winds, 75
Three Guineas, 43
"To Be Young, Gifted and Black," 59, 60
To the Lighthouse, 41, 43
To Stay Alive, 117
Tony Awards, 91
Tripmaster Monkey—His Fake Book, 103
True Stories, 91
Twentieth-century literature, 11
Two Schools of Thought, 131
Tyler, Anne, 139–143

Uncle Tom's Cabin, 10
Undset, Sigrid, 12

Van Daan family, 47, 48, 49
Vindication of the Rights of Woman, A, 10
Voyage Out, The, 40

Wake of Jamey Foster, The, 91
Warhol, Andy, 97, 98
Waves, The, 42–43
Westmacott, Mary. *See* Christie, Agatha
Westminster Review, 26, 27
Wharton, Edith, 12
What Use Are Flowers?, 59
Wollstonecraft, Mary, 10
Women and the Men, The, 75
Woman Warrior, The, 103
Woman Writer: Occasions & Opportunities, 127
Woolf, Leonard, 40, 41, 42, 43
Woolf, Virginia, 8, 15, 37–43, 106
Writing
  advice, 62–63, 72, 81, 88, 94, 95, 100–101, 106, 112–113, 115, 118, 125, 129, 135, 136–137, 143
  block, 85–86, 136, 142
  choosing, 4–6, 9–11, 14–15, 65–66, 75–76, 83–84, 91–92, 97, 103, 109–110, 117–118, 121–122, 127, 131–132, 139–140, 146–147
  creative process, 77, 99, 104–105, 140–141, 142
  criticism, 79, 100, 119, 124, 134–135
  deadlines, 67, 68–69, 85
  developing skills, 147–151
  discipline, 69, 99
  editors, 70, 85–86, 100, 101, 112, 122, 133–134
  education and, 62, 78–79, 129, 132–133, 149–151
  influences, 14–15, 79, 129, 141–142
  personality and, 69, 156–159
  process, 5, 77, 84–85, 105, 128, 152–154
  reading and, 62, 72, 78, 81, 83–89, 88, 125, 129, 143, 150–151
  rejection, 95, 101, 106, 128
  style, 67, 77–78
  tools, 93, 99, 141
  types of, 154–155

Years, The, 43
You Must Remember This, 127

About the Author

Lucinda Irwin Smith is a graduate of UCLA and a native of Los Angeles. She is the author of *Growing Up Female: New Challenges, New Choices,* about the many options available for young women today. She is also the author of seventeen special edition magazines on fitness, personal problems, fashion, and beauty. She has written extensively about architecture and design, and is the author of *Movie Palaces,* a book about the lavishly decorated theaters of the 1920s and 1930s, with photographs by Ave Pildas. Because of her work during the Gary Gilmore trial, she was interviewed by Norman Mailer and was consequently mentioned in the later chapters of his Pulitzer Prize–winning *The Executioner's Song.* Lucinda Smith is a member of PEN.